Lovers' Light
A History of Minot's Ledge Lighthouse

By Jeremy D'Entremont

© Copyright 2015
All rights reserved

Published by:
Coastlore Media
P.O. Box 8491
Portsmouth, NH 03802-8491

ISBN-13: 978-1497493179

ISBN-10: 149749317X

Lovers' Light: Minot's Ledge Lighthouse

Dedicated to the memory of Edward Rowe Snow
The extraordinary historian and storyteller
Inspiration to countless students of maritime history

Acknowledgements

Minot's Ledge Lighthouse has inspired countless writers and historians over the past century and a half. I want to thank everyone who has navigated these same waters before me, particularly Elinor De Wire, Bob Fraser, J. Candace Clifford, David Wadsworth, Arthur Richmond, and the legendary maritime historian Edward Rowe Snow. It was the passion and influence of Mr. Snow that led me to a deep fascination with lighthouses, and especially this one.

Mr. Snow's daughter, Dolly Bicknell, has been a constant source of support and friendship. I also wish to express my gratitude to the Cohasset Historical Society, the Scituate Historical Society, the Coast Guard Historian's Office, the American Lighthouse Foundation, the U.S. Lighthouse Society, the National Archives, and the Library of Congress. Many thanks to my friends Ed and Bobbie Stevenson and to my brother Jim D'Entremont for their invaluable proofreading. As always, I'm eternally grateful for the support and understanding of my wife, Charlotte Raczkowski.

And to all my friends in the lighthouse world, thank you for guiding me to safe harbor, again and again.

Jeremy D'Entremont
Portsmouth, New Hampshire
January 2015

I: The call for a light

It's not the tallest or the oldest lighthouse in Massachusetts, and few would claim it's the prettiest. But this sturdy, steadfast, wave-swept tower has probably sparked more imaginations—and possibly more romances—than any beacon in the state.

Minot's Ledge—about a mile offshore, near the border between the South Shore towns of Cohasset and Scituate—is a 25-foot-wide rock ledge that is part of the dangerous Cohasset Rocks, formerly known as the Conyhasset or Quonahassit after a local Indian tribe. The reef extends for some two miles along the coast.

It's said that the Quonahassit people would visit the ledges and leave gifts of arrowheads, beads, and various trinkets, in an effort to appease the spirit they believed resided in the rocks. If the spirit became angry, they thought, it would bring destructive storms to the tribe.

The origin of the name of Minot's Ledge isn't clear. According to the historian Edward Rowe Snow, it was probably named for George Minot, who owned T Wharf in Boston in the mid-1700s. Snow speculated that a ship owned by Minot might have been wrecked on the ledge.

The roll call of shipwrecks through the years near the Cohasset Rocks—especially Minot's Ledge—was lengthy, and many lives were lost. Local historian Robert Fraser has cited the wreck of the ship *Mary* on January 22, 1683, as the first recorded disaster on the ledge. It was closely followed by many others, some involving loss of life.

One of the more prominent shipping disasters in the vicinity occurred late at night on February 12, 1793. The 400-ton ship *Gertrude Maria*, bound from Copenhagen to Boston, ran into small, rocky Brush Island, near Minot's Ledge. Two men tried to reach shore in a lifeboat, but the boat was driven against the ship and one of the men drowned.

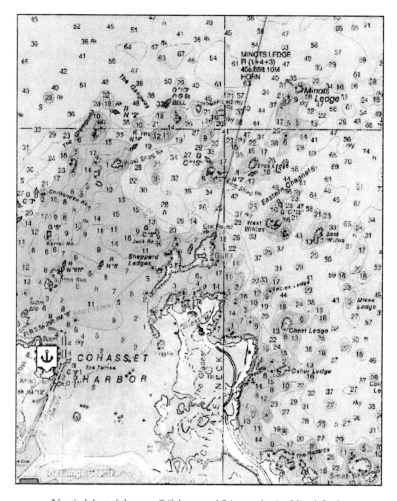

Nautical chart of the area off Cohasset and Scituate, showing Minot's Ledge.

The crew managed to clamber across a spar to the rocks, as the ship broke apart. The 21 men huddled together until morning, when they were rescued by Cohasset residents who launched their boats in heavy seas. The captain told the king of Denmark what had happened, and 14 medals were sent to the valiant lifesavers of Cohasset.

A Cohasset man named Joel Willcutt recorded some of the nineteenth century wrecks in his diary:

September 1, 1815: Last night there was a vessel sunk off Cohasset Rocks and five men drowned. Two were taken off the rock alive after remaining on her spars eleven hours.

December 6, 1818: A gale of wind S.E.; this morning there was a barque from Russia named Sarah & Susan loaded with hemp and iron, on Minot Ledge. At eight o'clock the upper part of the ship parted from the bottom and drifted to leeward with the crew hanging thereon. At one o'clock nine were taken off, four others having been drowned.

The salvaging of goods from wrecked ships for profit, known as wrecking, was big business in the vicinity. Underwriters in Boston employed local agents to try to save cargoes before the wreckers got to them.

In August 1838 the Boston Marine Society appointed a committee of three to study the feasibility of a lighthouse on the ledge. The committee reported in November 1838:

The practibility of building a Light house on it that will withstand the force of the sea does not admit of a doubt—the importance of having a light house on a rock so dangerous to the navigation of Boston, on which so many lives, & so much property has been lost is too well known to need comment.

The Marine Society repeatedly petitioned Congress for a lighthouse between 1839 and 1841, with no positive results.

In lieu of a lighthouse, minor aids to navigation were placed on the ledge. A wooden spar buoy was installed in 1839. A wooden mast installed in 1841 was soon swept away. It was replaced by a small, unlighted, stone marker that stood for eight years.

Scituate Light, established in 1812, was intended to guide mariners past the dangers in the area, but there was widespread feeling that it actually made matters worse; mariners often confused the light at Scituate with Boston Light, disaster being the result.

The civil engineer I W P. Lewis made reference to the problem in his seminal 1843 report to Congress:

For a long series of years, petitions have been presented to Congress, from the citizens of Boston, for erecting a light-house on these dreadful rocks, but no action has ever yet been taken upon the subject. One of the causes of frequent shipwrecks on these rocks has been the light-house at Scituate, four miles to the leeward of the reef, which has been repeatedly mistaken for Boston light, and thus caused the death of many a brave seaman and the loss of large amounts of property. Not a winter passes without one or more of these fearful accidents occurring. . . . One of the most interesting objects of this inspection was to ascertain the feasibility of erecting a light-house on the extremity of the Cohasset reef; and it was found that, though formidable difficulties would embarrass the undertaking, still they were not greater than such as were successfully triumphed over by a "Smeaton" or a "Stevenson."

Lewis was referring to John Smeaton, builder of the 1759 lighthouse on the treacherous Eddystone Rocks off Cornwall, England, and to Robert Stevenson, who was largely responsible for the construction of Bell Rock Lighthouse (1811) off the east coast of Scotland.

The towers at Eddystone and Bell Rock—both constructed of interlocking granite blocks—were among the earliest and sturdiest waveswept lighthouses in the world.

Lewis's report listed more than 40 vessels that had been lost on the ledge from 1832 to 1841. He asserted, "A light house on this reef is more required than on any part of the seaboard of New England."

Alexander Parris, a noted architect whose work included the Quincy Market building in Boston and several lighthouses—Maine's rugged 1839 granite tower at Saddleback Ledge among them—completed a survey of Minot's Ledge in 1845.

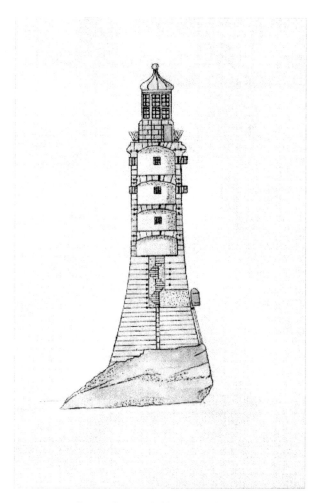

Smeaton's 1759 Eddystone Lighthouse

Parris recommended a granite tower, to be built "of the best materials and workmanship to ensure durability." He suggested an adaptation of his (unused) 1838 plan for a lighthouse at Whaleback Ledge at the mouth of the Piscataqua

River, on the approach to Portsmouth, New Hampshire. The high expense and engineering challenge of constructing such a tower in an exposed location meant the project was deferred.

The ledge remained unmarked, and vessels continued to have trouble negotiating the area. On February 12, 1847, a brig from New Orleans struck the rocks in the vicinity of Minot's Ledge. Luckily, the ship was able to make it to Boston with nine feet of water in its hold.

That spring, research by Captain Daniel T. Lothrop of Cohasset revealed that more than 30 ships had been wrecked in the previous 30 years at Minot's Ledge, with the loss of $364,000 worth of property and about 40 lives.

II: The building of the first tower and the wreck of the Saint John

Less than a month after the wreck of the New Orleans ship, in March 1847, Congress finally appropriated $20,000 for a lighthouse on Minot's Ledge. An additional $19,500 would eventually be needed for the completion of the project, including $4,500 for the lighting apparatus. The part of Minot's Ledge selected for the lighthouse was the rock known as the Outer Minot.

Many people believed a granite tower similar to the waveswept lighthouses of the British Isles to be the proper solution, as Parris had suggested, but Capt. William H. Swift of the Corps of Topographical Engineers deemed it impractical to build such a tower on the small (about 25 feet wide, by his calculations), mostly submerged ledge.

Swift had been born in Taunton, Massachusetts, in 1800, and he had entered the military academy at West Point at the age of 13. After graduation he worked in the Topographical Engineers as a surveyor of military installations, waterways, harbors, and railroads. He was credited, in the early 1830s, with creating the first comprehensive map of postal routes in the United States. He would eventually earn a masters degree at Harvard University in 1853.

Before his involvement with Minot's Ledge Light, in 1843, Swift had designed an unmanned iron pile beacon at the entrance to Black Rock Harbor in Connecticut. The structure had successfully withstood the elements in a location where three stone beacons had previously been destroyed by the violence of the seas.

Swift's 1843 Black Rock Harbor Beacon

Swift planned a similar iron pile lighthouse at Minot's Ledge, a 70-foot-tall, spidery structure with piles drilled into the rock, on the theory that waves would pass harmlessly through the structure. Swift explained his ideas in a report to the Chief of Topographical Engineers in April 1847:

As this position was examined principally in reference to a light house erected upon the principle of the Iron pile, it was not considered necessary to make an estimate of the cost by erecting a stone tower, which it may be remarked may readily be done, if it should be considered expedient, this however would involve an expense of from five to ten times the amount of the present appropriation while an Iron pile, it is believed , can be put up within the sum now appropriated, and instead of two or more years which would be required to put up a stone structure, the Iron pile may be erected in a single season.

The plan which I would recommend as a suitable one for this locality then is known by the name of the Iron pile light, a modification of Mitchell's screw pile light, several of which have already been erected in England.

The cost-conscious lighthouse administrators of the day appreciated the fact that a tower of this type would be far less expensive than one made of stone.

A prominent steamship captain offered the opinion that such a lighthouse would never last at Minot's Ledge, particularly when encrusted with the ice of winter. Many local merchants and mariners shared that opinion.

Swift, in an article he wrote later in January 1851, defended the decision to build an iron pile lighthouse rather than a stone one:

From the manner in which the Minot has been discussed of late, one might suppose the principle of supporting a light on piles to be new, and that the attempt in the case of the work in question had been a rash experiment, undertaken without precedent; to many it is of course known that, on the coast of England, the screw-pile light has been in successful operation some ten or twelve years, and although the construction of the Minot differs somewhat from the English, substantially it may be considered nearly the same thing, the essential principle requiring that the sea shall have no other obstruction in its passage beneath the light than as may be caused by the piles which support the superstructure. . .

The question has been asked, why put up such a structure in a situation so exposed—why not build it of stone? The reply is obvious: such lights can be built at comparatively a small cost, and in most situations in a short period of time. If we would emulate the English or the French, and would build stone towers like the Cordouan, the Eddystone, Bell Rock, or Skerryvore &c., we must be prepared to pay for such magnificent structures; that is to say, while the simple and rapidly-constructed screw pile may cost from $30,000 to $50,000, the great works enumerated have cost from $250,000, the least, to $500,000, the greatest, and the last built. It is very clear that, while we might indulge ourselves in one or two of these magnificent works, we could not undertake to build many, notwithstanding new light-houses are required on dangerous reefs and ledges at this time.

Work began in the summer of 1847. A schooner transported workers and materials to the site, and the workers slept on the vessel each night. A drill, which required four men to operate, was supported on a wooden platform. The contractor on the project was Benjamin Pomeroy, called by the *Boston Journal* "a person of the most extraordinary perseverance and inexhaustible ingenuity."

James Sullivan Savage, who had built Boston's Bunker Hill Monument, oversaw the drilling operations. The drilling equipment was twice swept off the ledge in 1847, and it took nearly two full seasons to complete the drilling.

A few weeks after work ceased for the season in late October 1847, the ship *Alabama* struck the ledge and sank about two miles to the east. The crew escaped safely, but the ship and its cargo were a total loss. Much of the cargo was later salvaged, and crockery from the *Alabama* found its way into many Cohasset homes.

The octagonal keepers' quarters (14 feet in diameter) and wrought-iron lantern (11 feet wide and 6 1/2 feet high) were installed atop nine 10-inch-diameter piles, cemented into 5-foot-deep holes drilled in the ledge and braced horizontally by three sets of iron rods. A gallery or catwalk around the living quarters, three-feet wide, was supported by cast-iron brackets. Some contemporary sources called the living quarters, appropriately, the "cage."

The iron piles were manufactured at Cyrus Alger's ironworks in South Boston. Alger was a well-known maker of cannons.

17

The 70-ton iron lantern was a 16-sided polygon, 11 ½ feet in diameter and 6 ½ feet high, with panes of French plate glass.

Drilling at the ledge resumed in the spring of 1848 and was completed in mid-August. All the lower piles were erected by September 21, and the upper parts were put in place by October 16. The cap on top of the piles was completed on October 30.

In November 1848, Captain Swift recommended that the installation of the lighting apparatus and the occupation of the structure by a keeper should wait until the structure had withstood one full winter's weather, and officials agreed with the recommendation.

In his book *Cape Cod*, Henry David Thoreau described passing the lighthouse while it was still under construction in 1849:

Here was the new iron light-house, then unfinished, in the shape of an egg-shell painted red, and placed high on iron pillars, like the ovum of a sea monster floating on the waves. . . . As we passed it at half-tide we saw the spray tossed up nearly to the shell. A man was to live in that eggshell, day and night, a mile from the shore. When I passed it the next summer it was finished and two men lived in it, and a light-house keeper said that they told him that in a recent gale it had rocked so as to shake the plates off the table. Think of making your bed thus in the crest of a breaker! To have the waves, like a pack of hungry wolves, eyeing you always, night and day, and from time to time making a spring at you, almost sure to have you at last.

Courtesy of Boston Public Library

Less than three months before the light went into service, at the height of Ireland's great famine, the 200-ton Irish brig *Saint John* was heading for Boston carrying more than 100 immigrants.

A Boston newspaper reported what happened on October 7, 1849, as the ship encountered a devastating gale:

Capt. Oliver ... states that he made Cape Cod Light about 5 o'clock Saturday evening, Scituate Light near 1 o'clock Sunday morning, then stood away to the northward, to clear the land, for about three hours. Then, it being about daylight, he tacked the ship and stood S.S.W. Weather very thick, he came inside of Minot's Light House, and there saw a brig lying at anchor, just inside of breakers, at a place called Hooksett Rock, tried to wear up to the brig, but found he could not fetch up, and threw over both anchors, which dragged. He then cut away her masts, and she drifted on to Grampus Ledge, where she went to pieces.

It was impossible to launch the lifeboats in the turbulent sea, and most of the passengers drowned. There were only a few survivors; 99 passengers and crew died in the worst disaster ever in the vicinity of Minot's Ledge.

Among those who observed the aftermath of the wreck was Henry David Thoreau, who wrote in *Cape Cod:*

As we passed the graveyard we saw a large hole, like a cellar, freshly dug there, and, just before reaching the shore, by a pleasantly winding and rocky road, we met several hay-riggings and farm-wagons coming away toward the meeting-house, each loaded with three large, rough deal boxes. We did not need to ask what was in them. The owners of the wagons were made the undertakers. Many horses and carriages were fastened to the fences near the shore, and, for a mile or more, up and down, the beach was covered with people looking out for bodies, and examining the fragments of the wreck.

The lighthouse was finished in late 1849. It was lighted for the first time on January 1, 1850, with 15 lamps and 21-inch reflectors in two tiers exhibiting a fixed white light. According to a contemporary document, the tower was 78 feet tall, rising 66 feet above the line of the highest water. Other sources put the height at 70 feet.

The decision to make Minot's a fixed light was based on the premise that it would be easily distinguishable from the flashing light at Boston Light, the next lighthouse to the north.

Minot's Ledge Lighthouse was the first lighthouse in the United States to be exposed to the ocean's full fury.

III: The brief life of the first tower

Because of the high degree of danger inherent in life at a wave-swept lighthouse, it was determined that Minot's Ledge Light would be a males-only station, with no wives or children living at the lighthouse. There were reportedly at least 50 applications for the job of principal keeper.

The first principal keeper—at $600 yearly—was Isaac Dunham, a West Bridgewater, Massachusetts, native who was previously keeper of Pemaquid Point Light in Maine.

There were usually two keepers on duty at a time; Dunham's assistants included his son, Isaac A. Dunham, and Russell Higgins of Cape Cod.

Dunham didn't believe the structure was safe. Only a week after the light went into service, he wrote in the log (original spelling retained):

Clensd the Lantern for Liting in a tremendous Gale of wind. It seames as though the Light House would go from the Rock.

William Dennison, an assistant to Captain Swift in the tower's construction, visited the lighthouse in January 1850. In a letter in the spring of 1851, Dunham wrote that he had told Dennison during his visit that the "structure was a humbug, and a trap to drown some poor fellows in."

Lovers' Light: Minot's Ledge Lighthouse

Isaac Dunham, courtesy of Dolly Bicknell

Captain Josiah Sturgis of the U.S. Revenue Cutter Service reported on the new light in a February 2, 1850, letter to Stephen Pleasanton, the Treasury Department official in charge of the nation's lighthouses at the time:

In all my conversation with Ship Masters in relation to the Lighthouse on Minots Ledge, I find it is the universal opinion of its being a very superior light. . . I think a large quantity of Granite thrown around will be of great service, as it will tend to break the force of the Sea striking the lower part, granite is easily obtained, and at a small expense.

Sturgis's suggestion of adding granite riprap around the lighthouse went unheeded. Dunham later compared watching a gale from the lighthouse to the spectacle of an army storming a castle. "You would see them in the distance, each battalion bearing the white flag, all with steady but determined progress marching for you!"

Dunham wrote in April 1850:

April 5—This day and the last night will long be remembered by me as one of the most trying that I have ever experience during my life.

April 6—The wind E. blowing very hard with an ugly sea which makes the light real [sic] *like a Drunken Man—I hope God will in mercy still the raging sea—or we must perish. . . . God only knows what the end will be.*

At 4 P.M. the gale continues with great fury. It appears to me that if the wind continues from the East and it now is that we cannot survive the night—if it is to be so—O God receive my unworthy soul for Christ sake for in him I put my trust.

April 7—Wind east with a tremendous sea which seems as if it would destroy the lighthouse, I pray to God to still the raging sea if it is his will.

Lovers' Light: Minot's Ledge Lighthouse

On July 2 Dunham wrote that his son, when leaving the tower, had to swing from a rope and drop into a waiting boat. "It would have frightened Daniel Webster," he wrote.

In his book *The Story of Minot's Light*, Edward Rowe Snow wrote that Dunham's pet kitten was so agitated by life in the unsteady tower that it jumped from the watchroom gallery to its death in the waves below. Fearing for his life, Dunham requested that the tower be strengthened, but Captain Swift assured everyone that it was perfectly safe.

Unconvinced, Dunham resigned on October 1, after 10 months as keeper. His two assistants also resigned. Dunham had offered to stay on if he could live most of the winter on shore as a "relief man," but his offer was refused. There were no immediate applicants for the keeper positions, so the authorities resorted to advertising in the newspapers.

The second keeper was John W. Bennett, a veteran of 25 years at sea and a former first lieutenant in the British navy who was described by the local lighthouse superintendent, Philip Greely, as "a man of courage as well as character." The yearly salary of the principal keeper was raised to $1,000, and the salary of the assistants was raised from $360 to $550. This was at a time when most principal keepers were making $400 to $600 per year.

A 640-pound fog bell was installed at a cost of about $200 in late October 1850, to be sounded in times of "fog and snow storms, or other thick weather."

On the ninth of October 1850, Bennett described his feelings about the lighthouse in a letter to the *Boston Journal*:

There has been much said against its security, and I feel that many statements floating about are false; although I desire to withhold my own opinion until I have snuffed a good strong north-easter . . . Much remains to be done to secure it from accident.

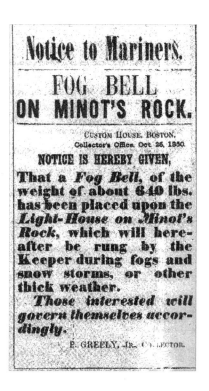

Any confidence Bennett had in the lighthouse's construction soon faded with experience. After a storm in the late fall, Bennett contacted Greely, who sent a committee to examine the structure.

Visiting on a calm day, the committee concluded that the tower would withstand "the strain of any storm without danger." The keepers were unconvinced.

Bennett installed a thick rope hawser extending from the tower to a rock about 200 feet away. A basket or sling was suspended from the rope, with the idea that the keepers could use it as an escape route in emergencies. According to local historian Robert Fraser, a special flag—a red diamond on a red square—was flown as a signal for a lifesaving boat to be sent from shore. Bennett did apparently leave the lighthouse via the hawser in times of heavy seas.

A visitor in late 1850 wrote in the *Boston Journal* that the lighthouse swayed two feet in each direction in a storm, which made it "quiver and jerk in such a manner as to make it seem impossible for the legs to sustain the thirty tons weight which rested upon them."

The writer was filled with "majesty and awe" at the sight of tremendous breakers from the top of the lighthouse:

Far as the eye could reach the sea was a moving mass of foam, waves rolling over waves and breakers towering above breakers, which tumbled in upon the rocks as if determined to hurl them from their place.

Bennett told the writer that he was the first man, other than the keepers, to witness the sight. A week earlier, one of the assistants had been thrown from his bed by the concussion of a wave.

Bennett and his assistants increasingly lived in fear of their lives as stormy weather became more frequent with the onset of winter. Assistant Samuel Gardiner described a December storm in a letter to Bennett, who was away:

During your absence we have had a very heavy gale and tremendous sea from the N.E. such a one as there has not been seen since the Light House has been built . . . . The house was shaking very bad from 9 am until 4 pm. The watch bell was constantly ringing and it was almost impossible for us to stand on our feet. There was a barrel of water standing in the cellar which was half emptied by the shaking of the house . . . . The piles beneath us are now one solid mass of ice nearly as big as a three barrel cask. As for the ladder, that cannot be found . . . . I assure you sir that it was the most awful situation that ever I was placed in before in my life, and I begin to think that the many stories which were told about it before I came were mostly true. At any rate it was much worse than ever I imagined it could be, and now sir you cannot think [it] strange that we are not contented to remain here for the paltry sum of one dollar a day . . . If we were sure of the wages being raised there would be some encouragement, but we are not willing to risk our lives for the present pay any longer. We do not wish to make you uneasy about our leaving, but we hope you will secure others as soon as possible who do not set such value on their lives as we.

Lovers' Light: Minot's Ledge Lighthouse

This illustration is said to have been based on a drawing by John Bennett.

A few days later, Bennett wrote to Greely:

My firm belief is that unless something is done and that without procrastination to secure the edifice more firmly it cannot stand and I fear something awful will happen.... I trust the Government will be led by your advice and influence promptly to adopt immediate measures to save the edifice from total destruction.

During a desperate night a short time later, Bennett wrote the following letter:

When I engaged to keep this lighthouse, little did I think that my heart, which has never for twenty-five years, in the most boisterous regions, failed me, would tremble at anything here. But there are things, I perceive, still in the background, to shake a stouter heart than mine; and so precarious is our present situation that there is a prospect that this may never reach you. These last forty-eight hours have been the most terrific that I have witnessed for many a year. . . . The raging violence of the sea no man can appreciate, unless he is an eye witness . . . . The rods put into the lower section are bent up in fantastic shapes; some are torn asunder from their fastenings; the ice is so massive that there is no appearance of the ladder; the sea is now running at least twenty-five feet above the level, and each one roars like a heavy peal of thunder; the northern part of the foundation is split, and the light house shakes at least two feet each way. I feel as seasick as ever I did on board a ship.

Our lantern windows are all iced up outside, although we have a fire continually burning; and it is not without imminent peril that we can climb up outside to scrape it off, which I have done several times already. I have a dread of some ship striking against us, although we have kept the bell constantly ringing all night. Our water is a solid mass of ice in the casks, which we have been obliged to cut to pieces with an axe before we could obtain any drink.

Our situation is perilous. If anything happens before day dawns on us again, we have no hope of escape. But I shall, if it be God's will, die in the performance of my duty.

P.S. I have put a copy of this in a bottle, with the hope it may be picked up in case of any accident to us.

A Cohasset man who spent some time at the lighthouse as a substitute assistant keeper around this time later reported that the bracing rods on the structure were continually being taken to a blacksmith shop in Cohasset for repairs.

Meanwhile, Dunham, the former keeper, wrote to Stephen Pleasanton, in charge of the nation's lighthouses, in early January 1851. Dunham said he was enjoying life at his landlocked home "mutch better than on that Rock." Dunham reiterated his fears that the tower would soon fall if nothing were done.

Greely, apparently tiring of the constant flow of dire predictions from the present and former keepers, wrote to Pleasanton:

The keepers are not very judicious, and are quite too much disposed to consider themselves heroes, and I do not know as if it is possible to prevent them or anybody else from "magnifying" their office and telling exaggerated and frightful stories . . . .

I have always said to you that, in my judgment, the Light House is perfectly safe . . . but I have thought it was best to get an appropriation from Congress to be expended in strengthening the House . . . and I have recommended also, in strong terms, an increase of the Salaries of the Keepers.

Captain Swift felt compelled to respond to the widespread fear that the tower would fall. A long letter from Swift was published in the January 18, 1851, edition of the *Boston Daily Advertiser* and in the February edition of *Appleton's Mechanic's Magazine*. There were worries that the rock had split where one of the legs was inserted, but Swift said it was a natural fissure that hadn't changed since the ledge was first examined.

A few iron ties had been added to the lower part of the structure late in 1850 with the idea of reducing vibration in storms, and it was intended that more such supports would be added. Swift was very much against this, believing that it would give more surface for the seas to strike during rough weather. Swift wrote:

[T]he principle of the screw-pile light requires that the least possible extent of surface should be exposed to the action of the sea; and while there is no question that the upper series of ties, beyond the reach of the sea, does stiffen the structure, it is questionable whether the advantage gained by the introduction of the ties below is not entirely over-balanced by the injurious effect produced by the continual striking of the sea against them . . .

The remedies which have been suggested for the supposed errors in the construction of the Minot are somewhat amusing. One is to build within the iron piles a kind of Eddystone, junior, vis: granite blocks secured to the rock. Rather costly it might prove . . .

> *Time, the great expounder of the truth or the fallacy of the question, will decide for or against the Minot; but inasmuch as the light has outlived nearly three winters, there is some reason to hope that it may survive one or two more.*

In his article, Swift expressed worry about the escape hawser installed by Bennett, calling it a "gross violation of common sense . . . . It needs no Solomon to perceive that the effect of the sea upon this guy is precisely that which a gang of men would exert if laboring at the rope to pull the light-house down."

Another storm struck the Boston area on Sunday, March 16. The keepers were awakened about 2:00 a.m. by howling wind and snow. The tower was swaying so violently that they had trouble staying on their feet.

Heavy seas smashed the dory and forced the keepers to spend nearly four days in the storeroom, below their living quarters, living on uncooked meat and bread until the seas died down. The violent pitching of the tower nearly threw the men off the ladder when they made their way up to the lantern.

The *Pittsfield Sun* reported after the storm:

> *Minot's Ledge light house stood the racket bravely; and . . . it may confidently be expected that the edifice will withstand the elements hereafter.*

As bad as it was, the storm was insignificant compared to what would take place just a few weeks later.

During a visit to Boston just after the March storm, Assistant Keeper Joseph Wilson, a 20-year-old native of England, visited the office of the *Boston Journal*. He described the ordeal of the storm, and a reporter remarked that it would be difficult to find men to keep the light if Bennett should leave.

"Yes, sir," Wilson replied. "I shall stay as long as Mr. Bennett does, and when we leave the light, it will be dangerous for any others to take it."

Wilson also said that in the event of a catastrophe, he would stay in the tower as long as it stood. He was confident of his ability to reach shore if the tower should fall.

There was another gale on April 9. Greely wrote a report a short time later:

The structure was not the least bit injured by the storm, and altho' the vibration was very great, I am inclined to think the Asst. Keeper's published account was somewhat exaggerated. The boat belonging to the establishment was lost during the gale and I shall furnish a new one forthwith.

IV: The Minot's Light Storm of 1851

Bennett went to Boston to see Greely about procuring a new boat on Friday, April 11, and was unable to return to the lighthouse the next day because of a strong easterly wind and rough seas. The conditions remained the same through the weekend, preventing his return.

Two young assistant keepers, Joseph Wilson and Joseph Antoine, a 25-year native of Portugal, were on duty. A friend of Bennett's was also at the lighthouse, but he obtained a boat ride to shore as the weather began to turn bad on Monday. Wilson and Antoine were left without a boat.

Increasing winds and rain arrived in the area late in the day on Monday, April 14. The *Boston Advertiser* reported that no vessels left the port as the wind was "blowing almost a gale." The *Advertiser* of April 16 described the increased intensity of the storm on the 15th:

The rain storm which commenced on Monday evening and which was yesterday accompanied by a strong north-east wind, turning into a tremendous gale last night, has created another extraordinarily high tide in this city and vicinity. The wharves are mostly overflowed, and the warehouse cellars filled with sea-water much fuller than they were by the recent flood [of March 16].

The *Advertiser* reported that it was believed to be the highest storm surge ever seen in Boston. Boats were used in the waterfront streets of Boston, which were buried beneath three or four feet of water, as merchants desperately tried to salvage goods from the flooded warehouses.

Many vessels anchored in the harbor parted their moorings. Trains stopped running as the tracks in many areas were damaged by the flooding. Telegraph wires were down all around the area. The tide rose over the bridges at Chelsea and Charlestown, and three or four locomotives were positioned on a railroad bridge between Boston and South Boston to prevent it from floating away.

The "oldest inhabitant" of Scituate said the tide had not been so high in that town since 1786. Several houses were swept away and the retreating storm surge left roads blocked by debris.

On Tuesday night around midnight, a Medford man named Theodore Locke was riding in his milk cart on Bunker Hill Street in the Charlestown section of Boston when the steeple of the newly completed Baptist church blew over onto his cart, killing him and his horse instantly.

At Exeter, New Hampshire, the flooding caused lime in a warehouse to burst into flame. It was said that the roar of the Atlantic at Hampton Beach could be heard five miles distant. The *Exeter News-Letter* also reported the loss of a boat holding eight people off Deer Island in Boston Harbor, but whether all on board died can't be known for certain.

Unable to return to the lighthouse, Bennett had retreated to the home he kept with his family at White Head in Cohasset. The house would eventually be flooded by the high tides of the storm, forcing Bennett and his family to leave.

The *Advertiser*'s reporting included speculation concerning the lighthouse:

Great apprehensions are felt in regard to the lighthouse at Minot's Ledge. The weather is still too misty to distinguish if it is still standing.

A former Cohasset resident, C. R. Kneeland, told his memories of the storm to the *Boston Globe* some 60 years later. Kneeland said that on the afternoon of the 16th, the platform installed on the lower part of the tower by Dunham washed ashore.

The light was seen to burn through the night on Tuesday, and the tower was last seen from shore, clearly standing, about 3:30 or 4:00 p.m. on Wednesday. Scituate residents reported that the light was last seen burning about 10:00 p.m. on Wednesday night. At some point, as the seas grew more turbulent, Antoine and Wilson dropped a note in a bottle into the waves below.

Lovers' Light: Minot's Ledge Lighthouse

The note, scrawled hastily on a scrap of paper, was found the following day by a Gloucester fisherman. It read:

The lighthouse won't stand over to night. She shakes 2 feet each way now. J.W. + J.A.

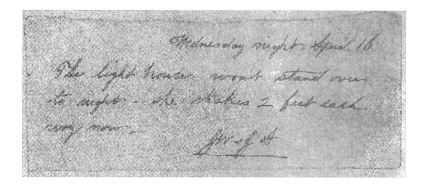

The tide reached its height around midnight. At about 1:00 a.m. residents onshore heard the frantic clanging of the fog bell at the lighthouse, possibly being sounded as an alarm or call for help. It was reported that the bell was heard from the Glades section of Scituate.

The ringing of the bell was heard only for a few moments. In an 1894 article, the writer Gustav Kobbé suggested:

No other conclusion seems possible than that when the tower heeled over to leeward each wave, as it swept over the parapet, struck the bell and set it swinging, so that the sea itself tolled the knell of the souls it was about to claim.

The central support apparently broke first; a man onshore reported that the tower had a decided list by Wednesday afternoon. The outer supports all snapped by the early hours of Thursday morning. Evidence suggested the two men left using the escape hawser before the lighthouse fell.

Nineteenth century illustration of the destruction of the first Minot's Ledge Lighthouse. (Courtesy of Elinor DeWire)

Bennett went to the shore about 5:00 a.m. He saw fragments of the lighthouse lantern and keepers' quarters washing ashore, along with bedding and some of his own clothing.

Bennett also found an India rubber life jacket, which looked as if it had been worn by one of the assistant keepers, but had apparently been torn from his body by the force of the seas. Two miles of beach were eventually littered with furniture and fragments of the wooden parts of the lighthouse. A second life jacket, also showing signs that it had been worn by one of the assistant keepers, came ashore a short time later.

Nineteenth century illustration of the destruction of the first lighthouse.

Later that day, local lighthouse superintendent Philip Greely issued a statement:

Minot's light-house, I am grieved to inform you was carried away in the storm last night, and I presume the two assistants were both lost.

According to an account in the *Farmer's Cabinet* newspaper, Bennett offered a $20 reward for the recovery of the assistant keepers' bodies. The body of Joseph Antoine was soon found at Nantasket Beach in Hull. The remains of Joseph Wilson were found the following October by John Bennett on a small island called Gull Rock, about a mile southwest of Minot's Ledge and only about 300 yards from the Glades section of Scituate.

The position of Wilson's body on the island indicated that he may have reached it alive but died of exposure before morning. Wilson's skull was fractured, suggesting the possibility that he had fallen or had been struck by wreckage from the lighthouse.

In their April 17 edition, the *Boston Transcript* called the statements Swift had made in January an "ungenerous sneer at the fears which had been expressed by Mr. Bennett." The *Transcript* article continued:

Had the earnest representations of the keeper been heeded, timely measures would have been taken to render the lighthouse more secure, or to provide a place of refuge for its inmates. But nothing was done, and in addition to the loss of life, the money expended in the erection of the lighthouse has been thrown away, and our shipping are now more than ever exposed to the dangers of Minot's Ledge.

The *Boston Journal* of April 21 reported that it was possible, with the aid of a spyglass from shore, to see that the central pile was broken off just above the area where the lower series of braces was attached. The other piles were broken off at heights varying from 4 to 6 feet above the ledge. The writer speculated that the center pile had broken first, and said that John Bennett believed the piles had been gradually weakening from the effects of storms.

William Dennison, as assistant to Swift in the design of the lighthouse, visited Minot's Ledge on April 22. The seas were still so rough that a landing was impossible, but Dennison was able to circle the ledge at a distance of about 10 feet. Some of the tower could be seen on its side in the water. The twisted appearance of the broken stumps on the ledge seemed to indicate that the tower had swayed back and forth before it finally fell.

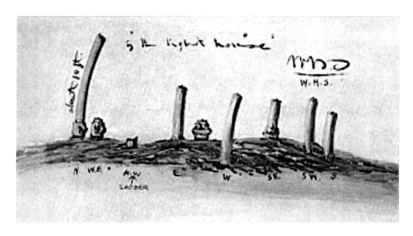

Sketch of the broken piles at Minot's Ledge, signed by Captain William Swift.

Dennison reported:

I could not see the slightest change in the rock whatever; the piles appeared to be wedged as firm in the rock as ever. I could see the heads of the wedges slightly projecting from the surface of the rock . . . The structure when carried away fell to the southwest, that is, directly towards the inner Minot.

Official records indicated that the fog bell was not recovered, but many sources claim it was salvaged through the efforts of a diver named Peter Fox. Dwight Faulkner, who was the owner of the Turner Woolen Mill in Turner, Maine, purchased it at a government auction in Boston. Around 1861, Faulkner put the bell on display in a bell tower at the mill.

The bell hung for many years at the mill. On September 3, 1905, a massive fire destroyed the mill. Francis Faulkner, who had taken over ownership of the mill from his father, rang the bell to summon the help of Turner residents during the fire. Faulkner became trapped by the flames and was killed, and the bell fell to the ground, suffering severe damage.

The broken remains of the bell were salvaged and recast under the direction of Francis Faulkner's daughter, Anna Faulkner Chase. The restored bell was presented in 1907 to the Bryants Pond Baptist Church in the nearby village of Bryants Pond, Maine. It remains in use in the belfry there today.

There was much debate about where blame should be assigned for the 1851 disaster. Swift's conclusions regarding the tower's demise were submitted in an official report on April 30, 1851. Parts of his statement were published in the *Boston Daily Advertiser* and other newspapers in May 1851. Swift was unsparing in his attack on John Bennett:

The light, as I am informed, was left by the keeper without a boat; and thus the means of escape were entirely cut off. I cannot say that the boat could have lived in such a sea; but, inasmuch as it was provided for that purpose above all others, it is certain that the course of the keeper, in leaving the men in the light without a boat, was entirely inexcusable, and even criminal.

After a review of the construction of the tower, Swift offered his conclusions.

The conclusions which I arrive at . . . are these:

First. That the sea did reach the main body of the structure.

Second. That the platform, or deck, placed by the keeper on the second series of braces, contrary to the design of the builder of the lighthouse, contributed to the overthrow.

Third. That the guy, or 5 ½ inch hawser attached by the keeper to the top of the lighthouse, and extending 300 feet north-west, or in a direction directly at right angles to the direction of the sea, north-east, had a most injurious tendency, and that it was enough of itself to cause the overthrow of the lighthouse, had the sea not reached the body of the structure. It is easy to perceive that the force of such a sea upon 300 feet of hempen rope of 5 ½ inches must have been immense, when the rope was attached to the weakest part of the building, that is, the lantern deck, 60 feet above the rock.

William Dennison, after his visit to the ledge around April 22, had reported that the feet of all the piles were still wedged firmly in the rock. It was, wrote Swift, "sufficient refutation of the often repeated story of the 'split rock'—this, like other statements from the same source, being entirely untrue."

Dennison also cited the deck installed by Isaac Dunham as a chief factor in the tower's destruction:

I think this deck or platform . . . should never have been placed there— and I told Mr. Dunham so at the time—as it was strongly secured between the piles, and would cause great resistance if the sea should ever reach to its height.

Bennett remained unswerving in his belief that the ledge was split at the base of one of the piles, and that the seam was fatally opened by the great storm. In a letter published in the *Boston Journal* on May 15, 1851, he wrote:

In answer to this I refer to Captain Morris and his crew, who, together with myself, have seen not only the splits in the rock which I have reported, but several splits from which large pieces have been thrown off. Their evidence will decide from whose lips the falsehood proceeds.

Bennett also questioned the quality of the wood used in the construction of the lighthouse:

Capt. W. H. Swift . . .very absurdly attempts to convince the Government and the people that the Minot's Rock Lighthouse was pulled over by a 5 ½ inch rope, or by the addition of a 3 inch plank platform. . . and in all his theoretical statements not one syllable has ever been said about the enormous quality of pitch pine employed in the construction of the store room, residence room and lanthorn [lantern], *specimens of which, together with one of the iron pillars and a piece of the rope, are now at the Merchants' Exchange, pro bono publico.*

Bennett answered Swift's personal attacks with vigor:

Had Mr. Swift made as great an effort in erecting a breakwater round the Minots, for the protection of his frail structure, as he has to shield himself from public censure, doubtless it might have still been pitching its inmates from one side of the room to the other.

Bennett also responded to Swift's charge that leaving the assistant keepers without a boat was "criminal," pointing out that a boat would have been entirely useless in the storm.

I wonder what course Captain Swift and his friends and backers . . . would have pursued, had they all been ensconced in the parrot's cage, with the little open boat, ready to be cast away into a sixty-foot sea—an old–fashioned north-easter blowing—and surrounded with ledges on all directions. The idea that a boat would attempt to reach the shore in such a contingency, was so outrageously absurd in the minds of sailors, that when I repaired on board the good old Forbes to read the news, her very iron sides fairly vibrated with the hearty laughter of all on board.

Bennett listed his conclusions in what appears to be a deliberate mimicking of Swift's findings:

It is the opinion of myself, and of many others, that the causes of the destruction of this costly structure are mainly as follows:

First. Owing to the disproportionate principles upon which it was constructed, there not being spread enough at the base to support the immense top weight.
Secondly. That the iron of which the pillars were constructed was of very inferior quality.

In conclusion, I would express my deliberate opinion that Capt. Swift was either incompetent to perform, or was very remiss in performing, the important and sacred trust imposed on him as a servant of the Government. By his neglect, or want of practical knowledge, my own life was in imminent peril, and my two faithful assistants met with a horrid fate.

Another letter from Bennett was published in the *Boston Journal*, two days later, on May 17. In it, he stated that his opinion of the quality of the iron used in the structure was based on his 15 years experience in a steam flotilla in India. He suggested that any interested person take a typical piece of ship's kentledge (iron used for ballast on ships) and lay it side by side with the iron from the lighthouse.

The debate raged on in the press. An article in the *Boston Transcript* cited a longtime shipyard worker from Cohasset who firmly believed that it was the heavy, frozen hawser that pulled the lighthouse down.

An article in *New England Magazine* likewise placed the blame in Bennett's lap:

The keeper's house and lantern were fairly above the reach of the average storm seas; but this was not the case with a lower platform which the over-confident keeper had built upon the second series of rods and tie braces, nor with that fatal 5 1/2 inch hawser which he led from the lantern deck out to an anchorage fifty fathoms inshore . . . . there are engineers who still maintain that a similar structure upon a larger scale, if built upon these rocks, would defy the storms of years.

In a letter to the *Boston Journal* on June 5, 1851, the former keeper Isaac Dunham entered the debate and placed himself clearly on the side of John Bennett. Dunham noted that William Dennison claimed that he had declared it a bad decision to place the deck on the second series of braces. Dennison stated that he had expressed this opinion to Dunham soon after the deck was installed. According to Dunham, the deck had been installed in August 1850 and the last time he had seen Dennison was seven months earlier, in January. Dunham went on:

The deck I had put on was approved by every one who visited the Light and ought in my opinion to have been placed there by the builder, for there was no place to land our supplies with safety but on the receiving deck.

According to Dunham, the original construction of the lighthouse placed a storeroom door directly over the ledge, where the seas continually broke, making it hard to land supplies. "To remedy this evil we put on the deck," explained Dunham.

Swift had a long and successful career after the Minot's disaster. From 1846 to 1877, he was the chairman of the board of the Hannibal and St. Joseph Railroad, and he was also a director of the St. Louis, Iron Mountain and Southern Railroad.

When he died in 1879, the other directors passed a resolution praising Swift's "high character and attainments." His biographer, George Washington Cullum, wrote of Swift's "gentle, cheerful and buoyant spirit," and his "devotion to duty as a shrine of worship," among many other admirable qualities.

So who was to blame for the demise of the lighthouse and its two brave, young keepers? The answer probably lies somewhere in the middle ground. Neither Swift nor Bennett received any official censure from the government, and the trust officials had in Bennett was demonstrated by the fact that he became the captain of the light vessel that temporarily marked treacherous Minot's Ledge.

V: The aftermath

The Boston Marine Society held an emergency meeting a few hours after the lighthouse's demise, to devise some plan to reestablish a light at the ledge as quickly as possible. The towboat *R. B. Forbes* was sent to display a light, but another storm on April 20 forced the boat to return to port. John Bennett visited the ledge on April 24, and a 31-foot spar was placed as a warning to mariners.

A short time later a small lightship, stationed at Brandywine Shoal in the Delaware Bay since 1823, was anchored in position at the ledge with John Bennett in command. The lightship crew had a famous pet for a time; their Newfoundland dog was renowned for fetching floating bundles of newspapers dropped off by passing ships.

An inspection report in July 1851 called the vessel "too small" and "dirty and apparently not well cared for." A new lightship, built for about $27,000 at Somerset, Massachusetts, served at the station from 1854 to 1860.

Gridley Bryant, a Scituate native and prominent engineer who had worked with Alexander Parris on the building of sturdy Saddleback Ledge Lighthouse in Maine in 1839, wrote a plan for a granite lighthouse on Minot's Ledge in the early 1850s. Gridley suggested that the rock known as Inner Minot's might offer some advantages over Outer Minot's. The

Inner Minot's, he wrote, provided a "greater facility in landing," and was somewhat sheltered from waves in severe storms because the Outer Minot's rock served as a natural breakwater.

1854 illustration of the lightship at Minot's Ledge, from Gleason's Pictorial.

Although Bryant's suggestion for the location wasn't adopted, it appears that his specifications were later taken into account. Bryant owned a quarry in Quincy, Massachusetts, that had been the site of the first railroad in the United States in 1826, with horse-drawn cars of Bryant's design pulling granite to a wharf. The granite used in the construction of the second lighthouse at Minot's came from the Granite Railway Company in Quincy and was transported using Bryant's system.

Congress appropriated $80,000 for a new lighthouse "of granite, iron, or a combination of both" in August 1852. Other nearby rocks were considered as sites, but H. S. Stellwagen of the Coast Survey considered them "objectionable as lying too far inside the outermost point of danger to serve with certainty in very foggy or snowy weather, particularly for vessels coming from the direction of Scituate light."

A survey by the Army Corps of Engineers revealed that it would be impossible to build a tower with a diameter greater than 22 feet without going below the low water line. That diameter wasn't sufficient for the proposed tower. It was determined that the diameter would be 30 feet, meaning that much work would have to be done underwater. According to the survey, the highest point of the ledge was only 3 feet 6 inches above the plane of low water.

Additional appropriations totaling $244,000 would be needed before the work was completed in 1860.

General Joseph G. Totten, chief engineer of the U.S. Army and a member of the new Lighthouse Board, designed the second Minot's Ledge Lighthouse. Arnold Burges Johnson, in his 1889 book *The Modern Light-House Service*, wrote that the project was "almost the first, if not the first, important structure attempted by the Light-House Board," which had been formed in 1852.

Lovers' Light: Minot's Ledge Lighthouse

General Joseph G. Totten
(National Archives Still Picture Records Section)

As the famed engineer Gen. John Gross Barnard later stated, "It ranks, by the engineering difficulties surrounding its erection, and by the skill and science shown in the details of its construction, among the chief of the great sea-rock light-houses of the world."

According to an 1896 article in *New England Magazine*, the "very table upon which the plans were drawn" was specially constructed from a massive piece of mahogany. A precisely detailed model, built in a scale of one inch to one foot, of the planned granite tower took two winters to complete in a Cohasset shop, and the model was shown as part of a lighthouse exhibit at the Chicago Exposition.

Lt. Barton S. Alexander of the Army Corps of Engineers, a Kentucky native and West Point graduate, made some modifications in the design and was superintendent of the project. A friend once described Alexander as "a man of massive stature, with a head and heart in full proportion to his body." In his later career Alexander became a brigadier general and worked on fortifications in New York Harbor, Boston Harbor, and the Maine coast.

Alexander first landed at the ledge in May 1855. He later described his initial impressions:

The stumps of the broken iron piles of the old lighthouse first attracted my attention. They had a melancholy appearance; they told of disaster, and the determination to remove them was involuntary. The wreck of the old lighthouse was visible under water, as we stood on the rock, and I determined to remove it also.

It was difficult to stand on the rock. It was covered with mussels and seaweed, but otherwise was much as I expected to find it. I examined it carefully, and measured it at dead low water in hopes to be able to report that we might get a few inches more than thirty feet diameter for the foundation; but I was disappointed in this hope.

On June 20, 1855, workers arrived to clear the ledge of mussels and to loosen the wedges around the stumps of the old tower. Alexander later described the challenge ahead in his memoir on the building of the lighthouse:

How was it possible to cut down this rock into any shape suitable to receive the foundation stones of the tower? Could it be done?

Lt. Barton S. Alexander (Library of Congress)

We could not land, even in the summer season, at times for weeks together; and when we could effect a landing, a part of the ledge was at all times under water, and the remainder only bare for the one or two hours at low water of spring tides. The space was contracted, and the sea broke with such violence during easterly weather that no coffer dam was possible. How were we to begin? What should be the process?

Alexander realized that if workmen were brought to the ledge in boats to be ready to work as conditions allowed, they would be idle ninety percent of the time. He came up with a solution to the dilemma by having the same men work on shore most of the time:

I determined, therefore, to combine the operation of cutting down the rock for the foundation with the cutting of the stone for the tower, and have them both done by the same party of workmen, to whom I could give constant employment and full wages.

A shore station for the project was established at 7-acre Government Island, formerly known as Doane's Island, attached to the mainland on the south side of Cohasset Harbor.

VI. The building of the new tower, 1855-60

After the ledge was cleared of mussels and the remains of the old pilings in June 1855, on July 1 a small party including Alexander and Charles Pratt of Cohasset, hired as a superintendent, again visited the ledge. Alexander used a hammer and chisel to make a benchmark at the highest part of the ledge. In the following days, the crew marked the ledge to indicate how it would be leveled.

Only 130 hours of work were completed at the site in 1855. The work on the foundation could take place only at low tide at times of calm seas, and the season lasted only until September 15.

Labor at the site began in earnest on April 1, 1856, with the cutting of the uneven ledge into a series of levels.

A permanent cofferdam around the work site was not possible because of the rough conditions, but the crew utilized temporary cofferdams around portions of the ledge using two or three hundred sandbags at a time. "These little dams only required a few moments in construction," wrote Alexander, "and, as they were easily removed, they were inexpensive."

A 20-foot-high scaffold was erected in June 1856 to provide safety for workers and to aid the laying of the lower courses in the tower. The scaffold consisted of nine wrought-iron shafts inserted into the holes left by the original lighthouse and rising to a height of 20 feet above low water, with the upper portion bound together by a wrought-iron frame. The sturdy posts were 10 inches in diameter at the bottom and 7 inches at the top. Alexander explained how the workmen utilized the scaffold:

This scaffold gave us some command of the rock, and it gave great confidence to new hands. By stretching lines between the posts across the rock in different directions, about two or three feet above it, every workman had something within his reach to lay hold of when a wave would break over the rock, thus doing away with the constant apprehension of danger.

A total of 157 hours was worked on the ledge in 1856. The project had a setback on January 19, 1857, when the iron scaffolding was destroyed during a storm. Alexander was discouraged. "If wrought iron won't stand it," he said, "I have my fears about a stone tower."

A bark-rigged ship with a cargo of cotton, the *New Empire*, had been driven ashore during the storm. A party involved in the lighthouse construction visited the wrecked vessel and asked the crew if they had felt any unusual shock indicating that the ship might have struck the scaffold. One sailor said that he had sensed some sort of collision, and red paint from the scaffold was found on the dark hull of the *New Empire*.

Alexander was relieved when it became apparent that the damage was caused by a ship, not by the waves. The rocks themselves were damaged by the collision, and the work had to start all over again.

A visitor described a typical workday for the *New England Magazine:*

Captain Alexander had constructed two large, staunch row boats, naming one <u>Deucalion</u> and the other <u>Pyrrha,</u>—for he was a droll fellow, full of dry wit. The <u>Deucalion</u> was painted red, and this was more especially for his own use, while the <u>Pyrrha,</u> a green painted craft, was to carry the men. We would watch the tide from the cove, and just as soon as the ebb had reached the proper stage we would start out with it, and at the moment a square yard of ledge was bare of water out would jump a stone cutter and begin work. Soon another would follow, and as fast as they had elbow room others still, until the rock would resemble a carcass covered with a flock of crows.

When one of the workers asked what the names *Deucalion* and *Pyrrha* meant, Alexander explained that *Deucalion* was a giant of Greek mythology who would pick up giant stones and toss them out of his way, and *Pyrrha* was the giant's wife, who ate them.

Conditions were unfavorable during the working season in 1857, and only 130 hours of labor were completed. The foundation pit was nearly completed, and four stones of the foundation were laid.

The conditions in the following year were more favorable, and the lowest stone of the tower was laid on July 11, 1858. The first six courses of the tower were laid in that year, and 208 hours of work were completed on the site.

The painstaking cutting and assembling of the granite took place at Government Island. Granite from the Granite Railway Company's quarry in Quincy, Massachusetts, had been chosen over stone from Rockport and Cohasset because it was considered "finest of grain, toughest and clearest of sap."

Government Island during lighthouse construction (National Archives)

The specifications required that the granite blocks be delivered in order by course:

That is to say the stones for the first entire course must be delivered in advance of those of the second; and those of the second course in advance of those of the third; and in that order for all the courses.

A 1915 article in the *Boston Evening Transcript* described the granite blocks in some detail:

The first two courses bore small resemblance to ordinary masonry. The stones were carved into irregular shapes in order to fit into or upon the levels that had been cut into the uneven surface of the ledge, and the lines of their junction formed, seemingly, the most erratic curvings. In the next twenty courses, all of which were nearly uniform in plan, each block was doweled to the stone below it by iron bolts three inches in diameter, and also was dovetailed to its sidewise neighbors. Each stone of the walls above was cut with a ridge on its upper surface, and the lower surface of each was so cut as to conform to this projection on the block beneath it. The Quincy granite cutters declared that such chiseling never had left the hands of man before; and truly there was need of workmanship of supreme excellence.

A team of oxen moved the blocks to a vessel that took them to the ledge. Strong Portland cement was used to adhere the blocks to each other once they were put into their final position.

In Alexander's words, here is a description of the lowest part of the tower:

There were to be two partial courses of stone in the foundation before the first full course of masonry. The form of every stone in this foundation had been carefully worked out by Gen. Totten; but owing to blind seams in the rock, and to an accident, to be mentioned hereafter, the number and sizes of the stones had to be altered. As finally finished, there are seven stones in the lowest or partial course, all having the levels of their bottom beds below low water, the levels of these bottom beds varying in depth from seven inches to two feet two inches below low water level, the last depth being the level of the bottom bed of the lowest stone in the structure. There are twenty-nine stones in the second partial course; of these, twelve stones have their beds below low water, varying in depth from four inches to one foot two inches below low water.

One of the problems posed by the project was how to make the lowest granite blocks adhere to the underwater ledge. Experiments produced a solution—the blocks were surrounded with a layer of thin muslin, which protected the mortar from the dissolving action of the ocean water.

Lovers' Light: Minot's Ledge Lighthouse

Government Island during lighthouse construction
(National Archives)

The foundation stones were also secured to the ledge using galvanized wrought-iron bolts, inserted through the stones and into the ledge to a depth of one foot. The stones of the upper portions were secured to the courses below with similar bolts extending seven inches into the lower course. Also, eight posts were inserted into the outer holes left by the former lighthouse, extending through the first ten courses in the tower, with the space around the posts filled with Portland cement.

A Boston newspaper reported that a prize had been offered for the most practical plan for a derrick to be used for raising the stones at the lighthouse site, and the winning design had been submitted by Captain John Newell Cook, a Cohasset man. Alexander described the derrick:

All the lower courses of stone in the tower were laid from an iron mast, which was set up in the centre hole of the former lighthouse. The machinery and rigging, which completed the derrick, had to be put on and taken off this mast every day that we landed for the purpose of laying masonry. It was of simple construction, and arranged so as to float in the water, so that all we had to do in "stripping the derrick," after our tide's work was over, was to cast the machinery loose from the mast and throw it, with the attached rigging, overboard. It could then be towed to the tender.

A newspaper reported that Richard Bourne, also of Cohasset "fashioned the perfectly running, flawless pulley blocks of lignum-vitae for specially built derricks which were the pride of the sparmaker's art." Power for the derrick was provided by a large steam engine called a "donkey engine."

Not a single man was seriously injured in the course of construction, although waves swept the workers off the rocks many times.

The following rules were strictly followed, as related later by Alexander:

1st – *No person should be employed on the work who could not swim, or who could not pull an oar and manage a small boat.*

2nd – No landing on the rock should ever be attempted from one boat. There must always be, at least, two boats.

3rd – While the workmen were on the ledge, a small boat with at least three men in it should be stationed immediately alongside the rock, on its lee side, to pick up the men who were occasionally washed from the rock.

Courtesy of Dolly Bicknell

Despite the fact that all the workers were required to know how to swim, a Cohasset diver, Michael Neptune Brennock, was hired to act as a lifeguard. When a wave hit, the men learned to hold on tightly to a steel bolt or rope until the danger passed.

Once a stonecutter named Reed didn't hear the call of "Roller coming!" He was suddenly in the water 40 feet from the ledge, stunned and going under. Brennock was instantly on the scene. As the lifeguard held tight to Reed, the other workers got a line to the men and tragedy was averted. Brennock later commented: "The new Minot's tower was almost an idol with me. I watched it rise, knew and handled every stone in it, and now I love to sit and watch it from my window on a stormy night, when it shines like a huge star."

A story involving one of the workers was related in Edwin Victor Bigelow's 1898 *A Narrative History of the Town of Cohasset, Massachusetts*. According to Bigelow, a local man named Noyes had worked on both the first and second lighthouses at Minot's Ledge. After some sort of minor altercation on the job, Noyes disappeared to parts unknown. He resurfaced during the Civil War as a Confederate naval officer aboard the *Alabama*. Noyes was recognized by Cohasset men aboard the clipper *Golden Fleece*, which had been captured by the *Alabama*.

On October 2, 1858, the cornerstone was laid and an official dedication was held, attended by the mayor of Boston and other local government officials. The invited guests boarded the steamer *Nantasket* with the intention of holding the ceremony near the lighthouse site, but rough seas curtailed the plan and the event was held at Government Island instead.

Mayor Frederick W. Lincoln of Boston introduced Captain Alexander, who said:

Now again we are erecting a lighthouse here, but this time of granite, granite piled on granite, granite to build upon, the earth's sub-structure; granite engrafted and dovetailed into the foundation; and granite the whole. To give even more stability to the structure the stones are riveted together with iron bolts, cemented into their sockets.

At first the men were nervous with the natural fear incident to their seemingly dangerous situation, but no accident ever befalling any of their number, and every precaution being taken for their safety, as they saw, this fear was soon dispelled, and they worked as cheerily as if on dry land; and you now see before you, gentlemen, the result of the labors of as fine a body of workmen as it has ever been my fortune to meet with.

So may it stand, that 'they who go down to the sea in ships' may see this signal fire burning brightly to warn them from the countless rocks that echo with the rage that oft swells from the bosom of old ocean.

The great orator Edward Everett—a former governor, U.S. representative, and U.S. senator—followed Alexander:

Well do I remember that dreadful night, when a furious storm swept along the coast of New England.... In the course of that tremendous night, the lighthouse on Minot's Ledge disappeared ... and with it the two brave men who, in that awful hour, stood bravely at their posts. We have come now, sir, to repair the desolation of that hour.

The year 1859 saw 377 hours of work completed at the ledge. The masonry was finished to the top of the thirty-second course, 62 feet above the water.

The last stone was laid on June 29, 1860, five years minus one day after Alexander and his workmen first landed at the ledge. The final cost of about $330,000—including two keepers' houses onshore—made it one of the most expensive lighthouses in United States history.

The lantern and a second-order Fresnel lens were put into place, and the lighthouse was first illuminated on November 15, 1860. Its light was 84 feet above mean high water. The power of the light shown by the lightship that had served in the interim was described by the *Boston Post* as "farthing candles" compared to the brilliance of the new light.

Just a few years after the tower was built, the engineer William A. Goodwin examined it and found that the granite deck at the lantern level had cracked. A new bronze deck, costing $12,783 and consisting of 12 sections weighing a total of 17,000 pounds, was constructed in 1866 at the Portland, Maine, facility of Ira Winn. The sections were hoisted to the top of the tower from a boat in heavy seas.

Winn had built the lanterns and stairs for a number of lighthouses, mostly in Maine. General Orlando M. Poe of the Corps of Topographical Engineers praised the new deck as a "superb piece of metal work."

Lovers' Light: Minot's Ledge Lighthouse

National Archives

Lovers' Light: Minot's Ledge Lighthouse

National Archives

VII. Life in the new tower

Built of 1,079 blocks (3,514 tons) of Quincy granite, the tower has stood through countless storms and hurricanes, a testament to its designer and builders.

The first 40 feet are solid granite, topped by a storeroom for coal, wood, and other supplies. The galley (kitchen) was located above the supply room. Above that, the next level contained living quarters for the assistant keeper. The principal keeper's quarters were on the next level.

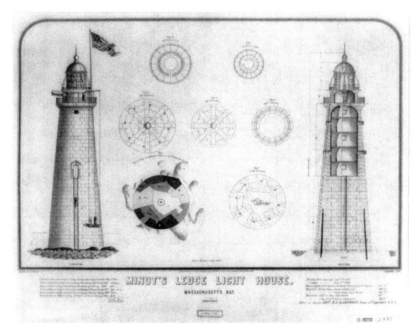

U.S. Coast Guard

Below the lantern was a watch room and space for the machinery that rotated the lens. The height from the ledge to the very top of the copper dome (fabricated by Boston coopersmith Erastus Badger) has been cited as 114 feet (or 114 feet, one inch) in some sources, although the nomination papers for the National Register of Historic Places puts it at 102 feet, 9 inches. The height of the focal plane—the center of the lens—is listed as 85 feet above mean high water.

Two galleries, or catwalks, were installed, one around the watch room and the other around the lantern. The fog bell was located on the lower gallery.

James Tower of Newton, Massachusetts, was in charge of the new lighthouse from November 1860 to 1874, with a starting salary of $1000 per year. Tower had assisted in the construction of the lighthouse tower and wrote that he was "confident of its strength to withstand the worst of storms."

The structure didn't always escape severe weather unscathed, however. According to Tower, the impact of the waves in a storm on December 27, 1881, "nearly knocked the chimney from the burner of the lantern." In 1863, a tremendous wind "moved the lantern, which broke off a piece of the manhole, above the watch room, weighing 15 pounds."

Tower reported that the sound of the wind around the windows during bad storms made a "continual noise like a locomotive," and in such storms the keepers sometimes had to yell to each other to be heard.

The tower never vibrated, but the worst weather sometimes caused a "jarring" of the structure. At such times, the keepers moved their beds away from the walls so they wouldn't be jarred from their sleep.

In 1882, Tower recalled his 13 years as keeper in an article in the *Boston Herald*:

Just think of it, away from friends, out of the world, in the very jaws of death, with nothing to do but an hour's worth of work a day in the lantern, except to play cards, checkers, etc., and smoke. The only chance to get air and exercise was on pleasant days, when we would play tag like children around the balcony on top. Each year I would test the strength of my nerves by painting the dome of the light. On pleasant days we would all sit out on the balcony, with our spyglasses in our hands, and watch the vessels go by, the shore and everything of interest. That was our chief amusement. One man of the four was always on shore on leave of absence. In the summer he was allowed one week, and in the winter two weeks. This was always eagerly looked forward to by all, and it seemed like being restored from death to life to visit the shore and one's friends. Weeks and weeks would sometimes pass without receiving news from land.

In April 1865, the keepers were anxiously awaiting the latest news of the Civil War when they noticed that passing ships were flying their flags at half-mast. They could also hear the distant tolling of bells and firing of guns. The men hailed a passing vessel and a man called to them through a megaphone: "President Lincoln assassinated."

When Tower died in 1888, the *Boston Globe* reported:

The hardship of such a life seriously injured his health and he gave up his position there and returned to Newton, where for the past 13 years he has held the situation of janitor in the public library.

The poet Henry Wadsworth Longfellow, whose many visits to Portland Head Light in Maine inspired his poem "The Lighthouse," visited Minot's Ledge Light in 1871. Longfellow was hoisted to the doorway in the tower on a chair, and that method of entry was thereafter known as "Longfellow's chair." He wrote:

We find ourselves at the base of the lighthouse rising sheer out of the sea . . . . We are hoisted up forty feet in a chair, some of us; others go up by an iron ladder . . . . The lighthouse rises out of the sea like a beautiful stone cannon, mouth upward, belching forth only friendly fires.

Surprisingly, visitors to the tower were quite common. Records indicated 710 visitors in 1861 and 496 in 1865. In 1937, 357 people toured the lighthouse. The youngest was

Mary Ellen Keith, who was carried to the top of the tower in August 1869 at the age of nine months.

The Lighthouse Board's annual report of 1867 reported that leaks in the stone deck at the lantern level had been repaired with a new "gun metal deck bedded in paint cement." The report stated that the new work was "in entire keeping with the grandeur and beauty of the structure."

Levi L. Creed was an assistant keeper under Tower from 1865 to 1874, and he became the principal keeper in 1874 at $1000 per year. Some people worried that the new tower would ultimately topple in a storm, like its predecessor, but in a letter to the *Boston Globe* in April 1876—25 years almost to the day after the original tower was destroyed—Creed reassured the public after a particularly bad storm.

I have the honor to report that during the gale of the 4th and 5th insts., the sea for hours dashed over the height of thirty feet above the dome; everything above the oil room was on the move, even the lens itself trembling violently. The sea broke on the ledge with such tremendous force as to displace a section of the rock, weighing in my opinion some four or five hundred pounds. Altogether it the most terrible gale I have seen during my residence in this light, some nine years. The sea continued to break clean over the lighthouse for ten hours after the gale abated.

The storm described by Creed was probably the same one noted in the Lighthouse Board's annual report, according to which a "section of the ledge itself, weighing probably about 500 pounds," was carried away by the sea. The lighthouse, nevertheless, was "in good condition, and well cared for."

Another ex-keeper in the late nineteenth century said that during storms, when high waves struck the tower, seawater would enter through the vents in the lantern, dripping down the interior walls. Anything movable would move about the floors, and anything breakable had to be secured. Still, keepers felt that the tower would survive any storm.

Levi Creed remained principal keeper until 1881. Parmalee McFadden, Creed's nephew, visited the lighthouse when he was 14. Years later, he wrote about the visit in *St. Nicholas* magazine:

If the sea is very calm, the more venturesome will approach the base and mount the ladder, which reaches some forty feet up to the first opening. If the sea is too rough for this, or when ladies desire to make a visit, the boat is made fast to the lighthouse's buoy, and the visitor is securely tied in a wooden armchair and hauled up by a block and tackle.

This precaution of fastening the visitor in the chair is especially imperative with timid persons or those who are at all liable to become dizzy; for although the chair is hung so as to give it a tilt backward, yet if a person fainted and fell forward, nothing but a strong rope would keep him from falling out of the chair. The rope is tied across from one arm of the chair to the other, very much in the manner in which a baby is made secure in its baby-carriage or go-cart. In winter, when one of the staff of keepers, who has been off duty on shore, comes out to the Light to relieve one of the other two keepers, it is usually so rough and the ladder so incrusted with ice that no other way of gaining admittance is possible except by being hauled up.

McFadden described the interior of the tower:

On reaching the first opening in the side, we came into the store-room, filled with fishing-tackle, ropes, harpoons, etc. In the center of this room was a covered well that contained drinking water, and extended down the very core of the otherwise solid granite structure nearly to the level of the sea. Above this room was the kitchen, and above that the sleeping-rooms, and the watch-room, where the keeper sat at night and constantly watched, on the plate-glass of the outer lantern, the reflection of the blaze of the lamp. There were always two keepers on the Light at one time - each being on watch half the night.

Frank F. Martin, after a brief stint as an assistant, succeeded Creed as principal keeper in 1881. Joseph Frates, a native of the Azores who was an assistant under Martin, was at the lighthouse for two tremendous storms in November and December 1885. After the first storm, which reached its peak on Thanksgiving Day, one of the keepers told a *Boston Globe* reporter that the tower didn't just shake—as it always did in storms—but actually swayed. Paint on the interior walls cracked and came off in sheets, and dishes rattled on the shelves.

The December gale left the tower completely coated with ice. Frates, who had traveled at sea since he was a boy, had never seen "such a heavy sea in such shoal water." Albert Burdick, who had been an assistant for 12 years, said he had never seen such heavy seas. The *Boston Globe* reported:

The light burned perfectly throughout the storm, but the work of watching it was very uncomfortable as the watch-room was cold and wet, owing to the heavy coating of ice. Captain Fratus [sic] *is firm in the belief that no storm can destroy this structure.*

Milton Herbert Reamy, a native of Rochester, Massachusetts, who previously served 10 years at Duxbury Pier Light and Plymouth Light, was the principal keeper from 1887 to 1915. A writer for the *Boston Herald* interviewed Reamy in 1888, and he was described as "on the youthful side of 40, with a curling bronze-hued beard and a clear, sharp eye."

Roscoe Lopaus, a second assistant keeper, served 20 years under Reamy. The keepers lived part of the time with their families onshore in two duplex houses at Government

Island in Cohasset, but they spent most of the time inside the tower. From 1887 until around 1900, there was a third assistant assigned to the station, making four keepers in all. At the time of the 1888 *Herald* article, two men were on duty at a time, each spending 14 days at the lighthouse followed by 14 days off. Bad weather and sea conditions often delayed the changing of the keepers, and it was not rare for them to spend a stretch of several weeks at the tower.

From the 1888 article

When it was time to switch keepers and the sea conditions were relatively calm, the men on duty would fly a red "liberty flag" to signal the keepers onshore that it was safe to make the trip. "I will say," said Reamy, "that one of the most disagreeable things about service at the light is the task of going to it and coming away."

Reamy was firm in his belief that the tower was secure, even in the roughest weather and seas. The jarring action of waves against the lighthouse occasionally caused slight variations in the flame of the kerosene lamp, requiring the keepers to make necessary adjustments. That, along with water coming in around the windows, was generally the biggest nuisance in storms.

Life in the tower, especially in winter, was more than some men could stand. "The trouble with life here," Reamy once said, "is that we have too much time to think." Legend has it that one keeper quit because he missed corners too much, as the tower had nothing but curving walls. Another keeper reportedly cut his own throat at the lighthouse, but the details are not known.

An 1892 article in *Harper's Young People* provided more details of life at Minot's Ledge:

Winter life in the Minots tower is very dreary. Its stone courses are so welded together that it has become like one huge piece of stone, and it sways under the blows of wind and wave as the trunk of a tree. But it as firm as the oak it simulates in form. The life tells terribly on the keepers. More than one has so far lost his mind as to attempt his own life, and several were removed because they became insane. In the summer, however, the keepers take turns going ashore . . . . Visitors often come off to the light. The tower is always well supplied with water, fuel, and food. The library of fifty volumes is often changed, the medicine chest is replenished, and the Light-house Inspector and the Light-house Engineer visit them at frequent intervals.

An April 1893 article recounted an unnamed ex-keeper's description of storms at the lighthouse. The concussion of waves hitting the tower would cause everything that wasn't fastened down to move; a pitcher of water couldn't be left on a table or it would be thrown onto the floor. Waves drove water through the vents in the lantern, sending seawater dripping down the inside walls. The writer concluded the story by assuring readers that "all the keepers are firm in their belief that no storm can destroy [the lighthouse]."

In September 1893, a *Boston Globe* reporter praised the hospitality and cooking abilities of assistant keeper Joseph Frates, who was described as "bronzed by the sun and wind" and was "as cheerful as such a fortunate individual should be."

Lovers' Light: Minot's Ledge Lighthouse

Most dumplings would serve well for paper weights, but those made by "Joe" were as light as the foam of the sea which swayed outside, and as delicious as if they had grown on peach trees, and had fallen from their own ripeness.

Jim Kingsley, another assistant keeper, dared the *Globe* reporter to walk around on the rocks outside the lighthouse at low tide. The rocks were, of course, covered with slippery seaweed. The reporter soon fell in the water up to his neck. Kingsley, who was "grinning like a fiend", helped him out.

The writer Gustav Kobbé, best known as a music critic and author of *The Complete Opera Book*, traveled to the lighthouse in the winter of 1893 aboard the tender *Geranium* for an article in *The Century* magazine. He described one of the keepers descending partway down the ladder with an axe he used to chop the ice away from the rungs as the boat approached. "He looked like a pygmy hanging there against the forty feet of granite up which the ladder ran," Kobbé wrote.

Because the sea conditions were too rough for the use of the ladder, Kobbé was hoisted to the doorway of the tower on the end of a loop attached to a line held by the keeper.

Straddling the loop, and grasping the rope above it with both hands, I gave the signal, and the keepers began hoisting, while one of the boat's crew slowly paid out the line to which the loop was attached. I was literally hanging between sea and sky, being hoisted upward and at the same time across toward the tower. It was a gray day. Where the sea below me shallowed over the jagged rocks around the base of the tower, I saw a tangle of slimy seaweed swirl halfway up to the surface and sink slowly out of sight. The little craft was now rising upon the waves, now lying in the trough of the sea, now backing toward the buoy, now moving away from it, according to the changing condition of the sea—and at Minot's it is ever changing. An accident to the boat or to the man who held the line attached to the loop, and no earthly power could have prevented my being dashed against the tower. But at last I had been raised to a level with the door, and was allowed to swing slowly into the arms of the keeper, who hauled me in, and was apparently as glad as I was to see me safely landed.

Kobbé described his initial impressions upon entry to the tower:

I found myself in a circular, brick-lined room, or rather cell, which received its only light through the deep, narrow door so high above the base of the tower that, as one looked out through it from the center of the room, it framed in nothing but a distant vista of heaving sea and gray, scurrying clouds. In the wall opposite the door was a small, deep window, like the port-hole in a casemate. Its heavy wooden shutter was securely bolted, yet water was dripping from the granite recess into a bucket on the floor, with such force does the sea strike the tower on Minot's Ledge. An iron stairway curved along the wall through an iron ceiling to the story above.

The granite floor was wet from spray that had been blown in through the doorway, and the roar of the sea reverberated within the confines of the room.

The keepers circa 1893

Kobbé stayed at the tower for a time as the guest of Keeper Reamy. He provided a thorough description of the interior, beginning with the cistern in the basement:

The well, besides storing water for the keepers' use, serves as an indicator of danger; for should there be a crack in the masonry, it would leak. The store-room is one of five stories above the solid base. Each consists of one circular room lined with brick, and has a deep port-hole. All the stairways in the tower are iron, and so are the ceilings, except that of the fifth story, which is granite, is arched, and forms the top of the tower proper. These rooms are fourteen feet in diameter. The watch-room, lantern, and dome are built above the tower proper, the cornice of which forms a parapet around the watch-room, while part of the bronze metal ceiling of the latter serves the same purpose for the lantern-deck. The lantern is framed in iron, and iron supports slant from the edge of the lantern-parapet to the top of the framework . . .

Over the store-room is the kitchen, where the keepers also eat their meals. Above this is the bedroom of the assistant keepers, that of the keeper being on the third floor. Though furnished with only the most necessary articles, there is little moving room left. Toilet is made at the kitchen sink, an arrangement which experience has proved to be the simplest and the best adapted to the circumstances. The fourth floor is the oil-room, where the nights' supply of oil for the lamp is kept, the annual consumption being about 875 gallons. The watch-room —the drawing-room of Minot's Ledge Lighthouse—is above this.

At the time of Kobbé's visit, the keepers kept watch in the watch-room from 4:00 p.m. to 6:00 a.m., divided into four shifts. The early morning shift, 4:00 a.m. to 6:00 a.m., was known as the "dog watch."

At the end of the dog-watch at 6 a.m., the assistant keeper, who also officiates as cook, prepares breakfast. This is usually ready by half-past six. The electric bell rouses the other keeper from his sleep in time for him to make his toilet. This is a very simple matter on Minot's Ledge—at least in winter. It does not take a man long to put on his clothes there, because, on account of the dampness and cold of the sleeping-rooms, he usually goes to bed with most of his clothes on . . . No one thinks of going to bed on Minot's Ledge in winter without a cap or other warm head-covering. By the time one is dressed—if putting on one's shoes and jacket can be called dressing—and has washed in the icy water from the well in the granite base, the breakfast is steaming on the table; and a very good breakfast it usually is, for Minot's Ledge is bountifully stocked with provisions. Good food and a pipe of good tobacco are the only luxuries that tend to ameliorate life in this tower. Breakfast over, and the dishes washed (neatness is of course scrupulously observed), the lamp is trimmed and polished, the lens wiped, and the lantern cleaned.

Kobbé was shocked when he first heard the thunderous sound of heavy seas striking the tower. Waves have been known to sweep over the top of the lighthouse, and Reamy claimed that a wave of 176 feet hit the tower on Christmas Day in 1909. Besides their own voices, all the keepers heard in winter were the sounds of the sea and the clang of the fog bell.

Not surprisingly, like many isolated lighthouses, this one has its ghost stories. Kobbé wrote:

For there have been keepers of the present tower who have affirmed that one of those who perished with the old lighthouse haunts the spot. Strange noises have been heard in the oil-room—sudden rattling of cans and clinking of glass, as if someone were at work there. Stories are also current of the mysterious filling of the lamp and cleaning of the lens and lantern. . . . One night, as the midnight watch was drawing to a close, the keeper in the watch-room, who had been brooding over the destruction of the old tower, quite unconsciously leaned forward and rapped with his pipe. A few minutes later he was startled to hear an answering rap from below.

The other keeper was summoned by a bell, and he claimed he had heard no rapping. It was said that the keepers in the first lighthouse communicated between floors by rapping on a stovepipe.

Legend claims that to this day, in dark and stormy weather, sailors hear a voice coming from the tower crying in Portuguese (Joseph Antoine's nationality), "Keep away!" According to one keeper, many Portuguese fishermen studiously avoided coming close to the lighthouse.

Kobbé also wrote of a near tragic accident involving the station's boat and an implication of foul play:

The boat that swings from the parapet eighty feet above the sea is lowered only in emergencies. It is remembered of a former keeper that when a small craft was capsized near the tower, he leaped into the lighthouse boat, cast off the lines, and let it descend at full speed. Fortunately, neither cable fouled, otherwise the boat would have remained hanging, stern or bow up, as the case might have been, and the keeper would have been dashed to pieces on the rocks; for, as it was low tide, the ledge was not wholly submerged. At one time a dory was swung from the parapet. While a keeper was letting himself down in it the wood-work in the bow gave way, and the dory hung by its stern, the keeper falling from a great height headlong into the water. Luckily it was flood-tide, but he struck with such force that he penetrated the water far enough to feel the seaweed on the rocks, and he suffers from the effects of the shock to this day. It was discovered that some one had tampered with the dory — with the purpose, it is supposed, of creating a vacancy in the lighthouse service, repulsive as the thought may be.

An article in a publication called *Old Ocean* in 1894 described a visit to the shore station on Government Island. The children of the keepers informed the visitors that their fathers had worked out a system of communication between the lighthouse and the shore, signaling with the dip of a lantern or the motions of a flag. By this time the men were spending three weeks at the tower followed by one week off.

MINOT'S LEDGE LIGHT-HOUSE, MASSACHUSETTS.

VIII. The "I Love You Light" and 20th century life at the ledge

In 1894 Capt. F. A. Mahan, an engineer with the Lighthouse Board, suggested a new system for lighthouse characteristics—the system of light sequences or color that makes it possible for mariners to differentiate between one light from another. Under the new plan, every lighthouse in the nation would be given a unique numerical flash.

As a trial of the new system, on May 1, 1894, Minot's Ledge Light was given a new 12-panel rotating second-order Fresnel lens manufactured by Barbier and Cie of Paris, displaying a distinctive 1-4-3 flash—a single flash followed by an interval of three seconds, then four flashes separated by one second, then another interval of three seconds of darkness followed by three flashes again separated by one second. The lens rotated on a bed of mercury, and the rotation mechanism needed to be manually wound every three hours.

Someone decided that 1-4-3 stood for "I love you," and Minot's Ledge Light was soon popularly referred to as the "I Love You Light" or the "Lovers' Light," an appellation that has inspired numerous songs and poems.

When the light malfunctions, complaints are invariably received until the 1-4-3 signature can be restored. The author of a 1962 letter to the historian Edward Rowe Snow claimed that a tragedy was narrowly averted during World War II, when the light was temporarily operated as fixed instead of flashing. The captain of a ship approaching the area was expecting to see the usual 1-4-3 flash. According to the letter, he was confused by the discrepancy but was set straight by a native Cohasseter on the crew.

Helen Keller wrote of passing Minot's Ledge Light on her way into Boston Harbor in 1901 after a trip to Halifax, Nova Scotia. Although she was blind and deaf, Keller often described things as if she could see them. She wrote:

The colors warmed and deepened as we watched the beautiful, gold-tinted clouds peacefully take possession of the sky. Then came the sun, gathering the mist into silvery bands with which he wreathed the islands that lifted their heads out of the purple sea as it passed. A mighty tide of life and joy followed in its track. The ocean awoke, ships and boats of every description sprang from the waves as if by magic; and as we sighted Minot's Ledge Light, a great six-masted schooner with snowy sails passed us like a beautiful winged spirit, bound for some unknown haven beyond the bar. How delightful it was to see Minot's Ledge in the morning light. There one expects to see the ocean lashed into fury by the splendid resistance of the rocks; but as we passed the 'light' seemed to rise out of the tranquil water, like Venus from her morning bath. It seemed so near, I thought I could touch it; but I am rather glad I did not; for perhaps the lovely illusion would have been destroyed had I examined it more closely.

The early 1900s saw some changes at the lighthouse and at the keepers' houses at Government Island. The duplex house occupied by the families of the second and third assistant keepers, called "ill arranged" in the annual report of the Lighthouse Board, was remodelled. The changes got rid of a "long, cold, and useless" hall on the first floor and gave each family three rooms on the first floor instead of two.

1906 postcard of Minot's Ledge Light, doubling as an advertisement for Boston rubbers.

At the lighthouse, the boat slip was improved, the revolving machinery for the lens was overhauled, and new fog bell striking machinery was installed.

Milton Reamy's son, Octavius H. Reamy, succeeded his father as keeper in 1915. Correspondence from that year notes that an incandescent oil vapor lamp was in use in the lantern, and the light had a rating of 77,000 candlepower.

The three keepers around this time each spent 20 days at the lighthouse followed by 10 days on shore. There were always two men at the lighthouse, and one was always on watch. Each watch lasted four hours.

The younger Reamy watched as American destroyers left Boston Harbor during World War I. Naval reservists were stationed at the tower during the war.

Octavius Reamy guessed that waves had cleared the top of the tower probably 10,000 times in its existence. Once a wave struck with such fury that the clockwork mechanism that turned the lens was stopped. Reamy left Minot's Ledge in 1924, when he was transferred to the slightly less turbulent Graves Light.

One of the assistants around 1917 was Winfield Scott Thompson Jr. In an article in the *Salem News* in 2004, Thompson's daughter, Carol Hyland, recalled visiting the men at the lighthouse with her mother. "We took the newspaper out to the light," she said. They also took pies and cakes that her mother had baked. "They would strap us in and pull us up," she remembered. "We'd run up, right up to the light."

The historian/author Edward Rowe Snow told the story behind this photo in his book The Story of Minot's Light:
"The craft which was rowed out to the vicinity of the light was owned by Joseph Lee, Jr., and manned by Sea Scouts. . . . They arrived in the vicinity of the Light at half tide. Since the boat was at times almost perpendicular, Larry McDavitt had a hard task keeping the tower in range on his camera. After the pictures were made the boys sailed the boat back into Cohasset Harbor. It was an adventuresome trip, the courageous lads handling the craft perfectly under all conditions of wind and water."

According to Hyland, her father and the other keepers once encountered German sailors coming up the tower's ladder during the war. A bucket of coal was dropped on them, and the Germans left. It was that experience that convinced officials the keepers should be permitted to have guns, according to Hyland.

Hyland recalled her mother's being very lonely at the shore station. Every night she'd take her three children to a window where they could see the flash of the lighthouse in the distance. "Do you know what that means?" she'd ask. "It means I love you and good night."

When Thompson got to spend time with his family at the shore station on Government Island, he would sometimes hitch up the big family dog to a sled so the children could have a "sleigh ride" around the compound. In summer, the dog was hitched to a wagon.

Pierre Nadeau, a native of Canada who came to the United States and joined the Revenue Cutter Service in 1913, became a second assistant keeper in the early 1920s. A brief newspaper clipping, circa 1924 or 1925, tells us the following:

Pierre Nadeau, second assistant keeper at Minot's Light, has been commended to Lighthouse Department for keeping light going three nights without sleep, while storm held Keeper Tornberg and First Assistant Fitzpatrick on shore, where they had gone for supplies.

Keeping the kerosene-fueled light operating at Minot's was not an easy task even with two or three keepers on duty, and Nadeau's feat of single-handedly maintaining the light for three nights during a storm is worthy of note. Unfortunately, further details of this episode appear to have been lost to the passing decades.

A tragedy led to the end of Pierre Nadeau's lighthouse keeping career. On August 10, 1925, the Nadeaus' three-year-old daughter, Doris, drowned after slipping from a seawall in Cohasset. This apparently occurred while the family was staying at the assistant keeper's house onshore at Cohasset's Government Island, and Pierre Nadeau was at the lighthouse at the time.

After the death of their daughter, Nadeau's wife, Ruth, felt a change of occupation for her husband was needed. "My father really didn't want to leave lighthouse keeping," Gil Nadeau said in a 2003 interview, "but did. Kind of broke his heart a bit, and after that he never talked too much about his service days."

Per Frederick Tornberg—a native of Sweden who was educated in Germany—was principal keeper from 1924 until 1936, when he left for the tranquil light station at Annisquam, Massachusetts. Fred Calabretta of the Mystic Seaport Museum interviewed Molly Tornberg Orr, Keeper Orr's daughter, in 1990. She explained that her father had been seriously injured in World War I and developed double pneumonia. His lungs were permanently weakened and a doctor told him to find a job that would provide fresh air, which prompted his entry into the Lighthouse Service.

Molly was six when the family arrived at Cohasset, and she said they were "just aghast at the beauty" of the area. She recalled her first visit to the lighthouse, when she was eight years old. Manuel Figarado (or Figueiredo, in some accounts), a local fisherman who frequently transported the keepers to and from the tower, provided a boat ride for Molly, her mother, and her younger sister, Betty.

My mother would pick us up one at a time under the armpits and push us to the ladder and say, "Go!" and we'd grab hold of a rung and start the climb. Betty was first, I was second, and my mother last. About a third of the way up there was a rung that was loose—it turned in your hands—and I tell you my terror was so great that I considered dropping off into the Atlantic Ocean. I thought it would be much easier to die than to go on with what I was doing. But my father was up above encouraging us, "Don't look down, look at the ladder, come on up." And he grabbed each one of us and pulled us in the door as we got to the top, and this was six and eight years of age, you know.

In this 1932 photo, Anna-Myrle Snow, wife of historian Edward Rowe Snow, is being hoisted to the entrance to the lighthouse. Courtesy of Dolly Bicknell.

Molly's favorite room in the tower was the kitchen. "It was cozy and warm, and had a nice little stove and the cupboards were all built around—they were round cupboards, and there was a gorgeous banjo clock hanging there, and I just thought it would be the best place in the world to play house."

April 17, 1936 - L to R – Historian Edward Rowe Snow, First Assistant Keeper Otis Walsh, Keeper Per Tornberg. Courtesy of Dolly Bicknell.

The way down from the tower back to the boat was as terrifying for Molly as the climb up had been. "And so Betty and I were tucked into this chair and tied in, and then it was pushed out the door swinging on a davit. And we were lowered to the boat. Well, I think my fear that time was just about as great as when I got hold of that moving rung on the ladder— you know, to be swinging in mid-air. And, of course, Manuel's boat was moving with the tide and we had to make contact but he was reaching up, and grabbed the chair, and pulled it down to the boat, and we got in."

Molly recalled that there was no electricity at the shore station on Government Island, and that much of the house was cold. The children had the job of polishing the kitchen stove in preparation for visits of the inspector, Capt. George B. Eaton. "My mother told us if we didn't keep our rooms clean and everything spit and polish, Captain Eaton might turn us out of her home," Molly remembered.

By the 1920s the keepers were still spending 10 days on shore between 20-day stints at the lighthouse. Much of Keeper Tornberg's time away from the lighthouse was occupied by the maintenance of the house at Government Island. While on shore, the keepers also had to tend four small local harbor lights, which they visited by boat.

Once, on an off day, Tornberg left Government Island with his wife in a small motorboat, with the intention of visiting the keeper at Graves Light outside Boston Harbor. A storm came in, but the Tornbergs made it to Graves Light. Communications were down and there was no way for them to contact their family. Word went out that the couple was missing, and there were newspaper stories that the Tornbergs had probably died, orphaning their children.

Some time later, according to Molly, the family visited a Finnish friend. The man's wife, who spoke very broken English, exclaimed when the Tornbergs appeared at her door, "Oh no! You're dead! You're dead! I have you in my crap book!" From then on, said Molly, "That was the family byword—you're gonna go in the crap book!"

A 1927 inspection report provides some detail of the lighthouse in that era, including the fact that a system of electrically operated bells was installed on each level so that the keepers could be summoned from the lantern. The report notes that there were 10 closets in the tower, each fitted with shelves and used for storage.

The fog bell on the lantern gallery remained in use, and the striking machinery ran for one hour on a single winding. The water supply stored in the tower's cistern was delivered periodically by a lighthouse tender.

The station was assigned three boats at the time: a 26-foot launch with sails, a 12-foot dinghy, and a 13-foot dory. The launch and dory were typically kept in a boathouse at the shore station at Government Island, while the dinghy was kept on davits at the tower.

Tornberg was in charge when the tower's seventy-fifth anniversary was celebrated in November 1935. As part of the event, William H. Wincapaw—the pilot who originated the "Flying Santa" flights to New England lighthouses—passed over the lighthouse in a small plane with Capt. George B. Eaton of the Lighthouse Service and several other passengers. Tornberg conducted a memorial observance in the tower as flowers were dropped from the plane in memory of Joseph Wilson and Joseph Antoine.

Also on the plane during the 1935 commemoration was the historian Edward Rowe Snow. Snow lived in the town of Winthrop, bordering Boston Harbor. The author of *The Story of Minot's Light*, which would be first published in 1940, Snow figured prominently in the twentieth-century history of the tower. He brought large groups of sightseers to tour the tower on several occasions, and he took several dramatic, widely published aerial photos of the lighthouse in heavy seas.

Snow was an expert diver and swimmer, and he gained some attention from the press for a dive from the doorway in the tower into the ocean below. "The height was not so great as professionals attempt," he wrote, "but because of the element of danger which is associated with the ledge, more attention was given the incident than it deserved." Snow repeated the dive in 1962, on his 60th birthday.

In February 1936 Tornberg and Manuel Figarado were on their way to the tower when their boat became trapped between two ice floes about 600 feet from the ledge. The seams on the boat split and it began to fill rapidly with water.

Anthony Souza, the assistant keeper on duty, witnessed the men's plight and telephoned for help. Coast Guard crews from Hull and Scituate soon arrived and rescued the two men.

Lovers' Light: Minot's Ledge Lighthouse

This photo, taken on July 16, 1940, shows the historian/author Edward Rowe Snow diving from the doorway of Minot's Ledge Lighthouse, about 55 feet above the water. According to a newspaper account, Snow's dive took place at low tide and he landed in water just a little more than seven feet deep. He repeated the dive on other occasions, including his sixtieth birthday in 1962.

George H. Fitzpatrick was principal keeper from 1936 to 1941. A newspaper article described the life of Fitzpatrick and the assistant keepers, Anthony Souza and Otis Walsh. The men shared the living quarters with a pet canary named Dick. (The bird's singing "gave an air of cheerfulness in the atmosphere of isolation," wrote Edward Rowe Snow.)

A birthday party for Keeper George Fitzpatrick. (Courtesy of Dolly Bicknell)

There was also a substitute keeper, Wallace Hodgkins, who composed a little poem about the lighthouse:

Mighty tower of granite,
Its base above the sea,
Neither wind nor rain nor hurricane
Trouble old One-Four-Three.

Because it was difficult to get regular deliveries of food to the lighthouse, the men relied largely on canned goods. During one bad stretch of weather, they were down to their last can of tomatoes before a tender arrived with supplies.

A well in the lower part of the tower, filled twice yearly by the lighthouse tender, held the water supply for the keepers. One day, while a party of young women toured the tower, one asked what the well was for. Otis Walsh tried to convince her it was the keepers' bathtub. "It goes down 40 feet," he told her. The woman paused and replied, "You must be out of luck when you drop the soap."

By 1940 Fitzpatrick and two assistants were spending 20 days in the tower followed by 10 days off. During one bad storm, Fitzpatrick reported that every fourth wave was higher than the tower. His wife and their 15-year-old daughter lived onshore.

Even during severe storms, Mrs. Fitzpatrick said she never worried about her husband. Having a telephone at the lighthouse helped the keepers stay in contact with their families.

A severe storm in January 1941 sent spray cascading over the lighthouse, leaving a 40-inch-thick cake of ice that sealed the entrance door. Two assistant keepers, Patrick Brides and Robert Hamblin, were trapped inside. The men had plenty of provisions on hand and were in telephone contact with the mainland, so they were in no particular danger while they waited for the ice to melt.

Photo by Edward Rowe Snow in January 1941, during the storm that coated the lighthouse with ice and left the keepers temporarily imprisoned. Courtesy of Dolly Bicknell.

A transfer of keepers was made a couple of days later, as Keeper George Fitzpatrick was hoisted from a boat using a boatswain chair, entering through a window, and Brides left the lighthouse the same way.

The Coast Guard was considering automation of the light by the mid-1940s. A report called the station "one of the most undesirable . . . assignments that can be given a man."

Early 1940s photo by Edward Rowe Snow, courtesy of Dolly Bicknell.

IX. Automation and beyond

The light was automated—and converted to electric operation for the first time—and the keepers were removed in 1947. The new electric apparatus produced a 4500-candlepower light. The fog signal was discontinued at the same time.

    Coast Guardsman Allison Gregg Haskins was in charge of the automation project. Haskins had served at Graves Light as an assistant keeper with Octavius Reamy, after Reamy's years at Minot's.

U.S. Coast Guard photo

In a 1960 letter to Edward Rowe Snow, Haskins said that the second-order Fresnel lens was carefully dismantled in September 1947 and was stored in a room in the tower pending further notice. A third-order lens was put into service.

Some time later, officials of the Boston Museum of Science expressed interest in the old second-order lens. Before it could be transported to the museum, vandals entered the tower and smashed sections of the lens. As a result, according to Haskins, it was shipped "back to the Boston base and it was destroyed."

A power cable from shore—installed in 1964 to replace a battery system—was damaged in a storm in February 1971, and batteries were again used until the light was converted to solar power in 1983.

The infamous Blizzard of '78, on February 6-7, 1978, damaged an access platform and the entryway to the tower, leaving access hazardous until repairs could be carried out.

A renovation of the tower was carried out in 1987–89. The lantern was lifted off by helicopter and subsequently cleaned, and about 40 of the damaged upper granite blocks were removed and replaced. The Gayle Electric Company of New Jersey, under contract to the Coast Guard, performed the work.

The light was relit on August 20, 1989, and a modern, acrylic 300 mm optic continues to flash the famous 1-4-3 as an active aid to navigation.

In 1992–93 the remaining keeper's house at Government Island was restored for $200,000, money that was raised by the nonprofit Cohasset Lightkeepers Corporation. The house contains two apartments upstairs and a hall for community use downstairs.

The remaining keepers' house at Government Island, Cohasset.

Today you can visit Government Island to see a replica of the lantern atop some of the granite blocks removed during the renovation. Part of the third-order Fresnel lens once used in the lighthouse is on display inside the replica lantern. A fog bell is also on display, restored by a local fisherman, Herb Jason, and his grandson John Small. Herb Jason had rescued the bell several years earlier, when it was about to be used for scrap.

A short time after the disastrous 1851 storm destroyed the first lighthouse, a writer in the *Lowell Daily Journal and Courier* praised the two assistant keepers who kept the light burning to the last. "They perished in the performance of their duty," he wrote, "and their memory should be preserved by a monument as lasting as the rock which witnessed their struggles."

No such monument was erected until, in 1997, a group of local residents began a campaign to erect a granite memorial to Joseph Antoine and Joseph Wilson. The memorial was finished and dedicated in 2000 on Government Island in Cohasset.

Under the National Historic Lighthouse Preservation Act of 2000, the lighthouse was made available for transfer to a suitable new owner. No applications were submitted by nonprofit organizations or government entities, so in June 2014 the property was put on sale to the public via online auction.

The auction ended in October 2014, and the high bidder at $222,000 was Polaroid chairman Robert "Bobby" Sager, a well-known philanthropist. The automated light and fog signal are still maintained by Coast Guard personnel.

Lovers' Light: Minot's Ledge Lighthouse

Selected Bibliography

Adamson, Hans Christian. *Keepers of the Lights*. New York: Greenberg, 1955.

Baker, William A. *A History of the Boston Marine Society 1742–1967*. Boston: Boston Marine Society, 1968.

Bigelow, E. Victor. *Narrative History of the Town of Cohasset*. Cohasset, Mass.: Halliday Lithograph Committee on Town History, 1898.

Blunt, Edmund, and George W. Blunt. *Blunt's American Coast Pilot*. New York: Edmund and George W. Blunt, 1850.

Boston Daily Advertiser, January 18, 1851. "Minot Rock Light-House."

Clifford, Candace. "The First Minots Ledge Lighthouse." *The Keeper's Log*, Spring 2002.

Cohasset Historical Society, clippings files.

D'Entremont, Jeremy. *The Lighthouses of Massachusetts*. Beverly, MA: Commonwealth Editions, 2007.

D'Entremont, Jeremy. "Pierre Albert Nadeau: Forgotten Hero of Minot's Light." *Lighthouse Digest*, September 2003.

De Wire, Elinor. *Guardians of the Lights: The Men and Women of the U.S. Lighthouse Service*. Sarasota, Fla.: Pineapple Press, 1995.

Eckels, Donald, and Robert Fraser. "Minot's Ledge." *Keeper's Log*, Fall 1995.

Fraser, Robert. "Minot's Light." Typescript at the Cohasset Historical Society, date unknown.

Gleason, Sarah C. *Kindly Lights: A History of the Lighthouses of Southern New England*. Boston: Beacon Press, 1991.

"History of Minot's Ledge Light, Massachusetts." U.S. Coast Guard Public Information Division. Typescript, date unknown.

Holland, Francis Ross, Jr. *America's Lighthouses: An Illustrated History* 1972. Reprint, New York: Dover, 1988.

Jason, Herbert L. "A Time to Remember Two Brave Men." *Cohasset Mariner*, May 1, 1997.

Johnson, Arnold Burges. *The Modern Light-House Service.* Washington, D.C.: GPO, 1890.

Kobbé, Gustav, "Life in a Lighthouse." *Century*, January 1894.

Lighthouse clippings files, Records Group 26, National Archives, Washington, D.C.

Lighthouse site files. Records Group 26, National Archives, Washington, D.C.

Marcus, Jon. *Lighthouses of New England.* Stillwater, Minn.: Voyageur Press, 2001.

Morison, Samuel Eliot. *The Maritime History of Massachusetts.* 1921. Reprint, Boston: Northeastern University Press, 1979.

New England Magazine, "The Building of Minot's Ledge Lighthouse." October 1896.

Noble, Dennis L. *Lighthouses & Keepers.* Annapolis: Naval Institute Press, 1997.

Old Ocean. (Selections from *The Youth's Companion.*) Boston: Perry Mason and Company, 1894.

Orr, Molly Tornberg. Interview transcript, August 29, 1990. OH 90-28, Sound Archives, G. W. Blunt White Library, Mystic Seaport Museum.

Putnam, George R. *Lighthouses and Lightships of the United States.* Boston: Houghton Mifflin, 1933.

Scheina, Robert. "Minot's Ledge." *Keeper's Log*, Spring 1985.

Smith, Fitz-Henry. *Storms and Shipwrecks in Boston Bay.* Boston: privately printed, 1918.

Snow, Edward Rowe. "America's Most Dangerous Lighthouse." *Boston Herald*, April 18, 1971.

Snow, Edward Rowe. *Famous Lighthouses of New England.* 1945. Updated edition (as *The Lighthouses of New England*), Beverly, Mass.: Commonwealth Editions, 2002.

Snow, Edward Rowe. "Fear the 'Ghost' of Minot's Light." *Boston Herald*, September 18, 1938.

Snow, Edward Rowe. *Minot's Light: 120 Years of Service to Mariners.* Quincy, MA.: Quincy Cooperative Bank, 1981.

Snow, Edward Rowe. "New Facts Trace Busy Career of Man Who Built Minot's Light." *Quincy Patriot Ledger*, October 2, 1958.

Snow, Edward Rowe. *Storms and Shipwrecks of New England*. 1946. Updated edition, Beverly, Mass.: Commonwealth Editions, 2003.

Snow, Edward Rowe. *The Story of Minot's Light*, 1940. Second printing, West Hanover, Mass.: Halliday Lithograph Corporation, July 1955.

Talbot, Frederick A. *Lighthouses and Lightships*. Philadelphia: J. B. Lippincott, 1913.

Thoreau, Henry David. *Cape Cod*. Orleans, MA: Parnassus Imprints, 1984.

Tower, James. "Wind and Water." *Boston Sunday Herald*, May 21, 1882.

Transactions of the American Society of Civil Engineers, "Minot's Ledge Lighthouse." 1870.

Wadsworth, David H. "The Strange Saga of the Fog Bell." *Cohasset Mariner*, April 28, 1994.

U.S. Congress. Condition of the Light-houses on the Eastern Coast. Rep. no. 282, 27th Cong., 3rd sess., 1843.

U.S. Congress. Report of the General Superintendent of the Light-house Establishment. Ex. Doc. no. 11, 31st Cong., 2nd sess., 1850.

U.S. Congress. Report on Light-house Establishment from I. W. P. Lewis. H. Doc. 183, 27th Cong., 3rd sess., 1843

U.S. Coast Guard District One Aids to Navigation Office, Boston, Massachusetts. Aids to navigation files.

U.S. Coast Guard Historian's Office, Washington, D.C. Lighthouse files.

Willoughby, Malcolm F. *Lighthouses of New England*. Boston: T. O. Metcalf, 1929.my friend Ed

CPSIA information can be obtained at www.ICGtesting.com
Printed in the USA
LVOW08s1504260115

424394LV00003B/708/P